NEW AND
SELECTED
POEMS

BOOKS BY MICHAEL RYAN

POETRY

Threats Instead of Trees

In Winter

God Hunger

New and Selected Poems

PROSE

Secret Life

A Difficult Grace: On Poets, Poetry, and Writing

Baby B

New and Selected Poems

Michael Ryan

A MARINER BOOK
Houghton Mifflin Company
BOSTON · NEW YORK

FIRST MARINER BOOKS EDITION 2005

Visit our Web site: www.houghtonmifflinbooks.com.

Library of Congress Cataloging-in-Publication Data

Ryan, Michael, date.
  [Poems. Selections]
  New and selected poems / Michael Ryan.
  p. cm.
ISBN-13: 978-0-618-40854-2   ISBN-10: 0-618-40854-1
ISBN-13: 978-0-618-61941-2 (pbk.)   ISBN-10: 0-618-61941-0 (pbk.)
  I. Title.
PS3568.Y39N48   2004
811'.54—dc22   2003067781

Book design by Anne Chalmers; typeface: Requiem (Hoeffler Type Foundry)

Printed in the United States of America

QUM 10 9 8 7 6 5 4 3 2 1

ACKNOWLEDGMENTS

Thanks to the editors of the magazines in which the following new poems first appeared:
American Poetry Review: Ash Pit, A Two-Year-Old Girl in a Restaurant, Ballad of The
    Four Last Things, Chronic Severe Incurable, Complete Semen Study, Distant
    Friend, Eschatology, Every Sunday, A Good Father, In the Sink, Reminder, The
    Others, The Use of Poetry
The Atlantic Monthly: A Dead Girl
Kenyon Review: Birthday, Flimsy, Tribute, Wings of the Morning
The New Yorker: An Old Book in Florence, Bunny, Extended Care, Outside
Ploughshares: A Version of Happiness
Poetry: Tutelary
Slate: Dickhead, Dream Pun on "Single Man" Before Marrying Again, God, My Other
    Self
Threepenny Review: The Music House

Some previously published poems, mostly from *Threats Instead of Trees*, have been
    significantly revised. Revisions of "The Blind Swimmer" and "The Myth" appeared,
    respectively, in *American Poetry Review* and *Threepenny Review*.

Thanks to Michael Collier, James McMichael, and Ellen Bryant Voigt for their sharp,
generous responses to this book in manuscript; and to Stephen Berg, Louise Glück,
Stanley Kunitz, and Robert Pinsky for their love, support, and help with these poems
over the years.

FOR DOREEN

AND FOR EMILY
when she's old enough to read it

Contents

FROM Threats Instead of Trees, 1974

Speaking 3
The Myth 4
The Blind Swimmer 6
Pastoral 8
Prothalamion 9
Hitting Fungoes 10
Letters from an Institution 12
Deathwatch 15
This is a poem for the dead 16
A Posthumous Poetics 17
House 18

FROM In Winter, 1981

Poem at Thirty 21
When I Was Conceived 25
Consider a Move 26
The Pure Loneliness 27
Where I'll Be Good 28
A Shape for It 29
A Changed Season 30
Gangster Dreams 31
Memory 32
In Winter 33

All the Time   34

Sex   35

FROM   God Hunger, 1989

Not the End of the World   41

My Dream by Henry James   44

This Is Why   46

TV Room at the Children's Hospice   48

The Gladiator   50

Milk the Mouse   51

Meeting Cheever   52

"Boy 'Carrying-In' Bottles in Glass Works"   54

Winter Drought   55

Spider Plant   57

Through a Crack   58

Sea Worms   59

The Past   61

A Burglary   62

A Splinter   71

One   73

Portrait of a Lady   75

First Exercise   77

The Ditch   79

Smoke   81

Houseflies   82

Larkinesque   83

The Crown of Frogs   85

Passion   89

Pedestrian Pastoral   92

Moonlight   93

Fire   94

Tourists on Paros   95

Crossroads Inn   96

A Postcard from Italy   97

Stone Paperweight   98

God Hunger   99

Tanglewood   100

Switchblade   102

New Poems

A Two-Year-Old Girl in a Restaurant   107

Outside   108

The Music House   109

The Use of Poetry   111

My Other Self   113

Bunny   115

Birthday   118

Ash Pit   119

Tutelary   120

In the Sink   121

Ballad of The Four Last Things   122

Chronic Severe Incurable   123

Mr. Pain Speaks for Himself   124

God   125

Wings of the Morning   126

Tribute   127

Flimsy   128

The Others   129

A Good Father   130

Every Sunday   131

A Dead Girl   132

Distant Friend   133

Dickhead   134

Complete Semen Study   136

Eschatology   138

Extended Care   139

Dream Pun on "Single Man" Before Marrying Again   140

An Old Book in Florence   142

A Version of Happiness   145

A French Café in Orange County   147

Reminder   148

Threats
Instead of
Trees

SPEAKING

I'm speaking again
as the invalid in a dark room.
I want to say thank you
out loud to no one.
I want to suck my cracked lips in
on the sound, as the sound
dissolves slowly like a man living.

I'm painfully grateful there's breath
to make noise with, and many words
have meaning. I feel lucky
when hello doesn't hurt.
On a bus, I could love anyone.

It's not terrible to be alone.
Last night I talked to a person
so haltingly I might have been looking
for a word that wouldn't change.
That made her misconstrue everything.

Did she feel what I thought she was feeling?
Did she feel me concealing
the pleasure that keeps me going,
as I circled that pleasure
like a dog around its master?
This pleasure, for me, is speaking,
as if words enclosed the secret
in myself that lasts after death.

THE MYTH

For a long time, nothing happened.
Then ancestors whispering, then fragments
of a forgotten life disturbing ordinary actions:
handling a stone, or bathing,
you might think of the brain as a diamond.
Even thought was clear, like watching your lover
explore the bottom of a deep lake.
Everyone became friends,
mirroring one another's most personal gestures.
The leaders said this happiness
is round like bowls, and devised simple rituals
in which touch wasn't a form of searching—
a finger's curving could articulate anything.

Still, some looked for damage
in the hard scars on our bodies.
They reminded us of the years of pain,
when anticipation meant only disappointment,
and any object we desired
would cut brutally through the skin.
Shouldn't we be ashamed?
Isn't this history we imagine
in that one's ugly movement
of his arms? Her clumsy legs?

Reverting to privacy,
we began to see less distinctly.
Sometimes, during an intimate talk,
you'd swear you caught your best friend
closing his eyes, as in sadness
at his own reflection.

So we tried exhaustion, swimming alone
for days. Slowly we noticed our bodies
becoming smooth and beautiful,
and the air seemed less necessary
the deeper we dove. Maybe
we forgot we were actually underwater,
forgetting, as we did, all harm done,
all we couldn't be for one another.

THE BLIND SWIMMER

We know he's out there,
swimming slowly, searching for corners
in the sea where the dark has rubbed away.
Each breath he takes takes him deeper
inside his mind where voices without sources
scream "Swim!" and even the ocean
is missing. Still, he swims.
The water fills his cupped hands
like breasts, the one constant in a crowd
of waves pushing him nowhere, the blue
salt glued to his eyes like braille.
What do his dead eyes say?
The body that keeps him buoyant is a room,
the pain would stop if he just walked out?

On the shore, our feet planted like roots,
we watch for a sign. Some of us yell
at anything: a wounded dolphin breaking
into air, the torn edge of a fin
mistaken for his hand. The ocean doesn't
stand for our common life, what makes us
need one another, but we still fear
drowning. So, safely together,
we wait for the blind swimmer
to walk out of the sea and say it's all right,
you can swim alone without seeing.
Some of us wait a long time.

I know he's out there.
He smells the ocean, doesn't he, that old
naked woman? She takes his tongue
in her mouth, doesn't her mouth open?
I hear him going under,

quietly as memory enters dreams, his dream
nothing I can imagine, tasting water so deep,
light is terrible and fish see through their skin.

for Thomas Lux

PASTORAL

The trees bending in wind like inflections
in our discussion of love, that widow

lifting her underclothes to show how lonely
she has been, and you do address her

if only to say *yes we're very different*
my husband is so gentle these evenings,

as through the window above our headboard
the animals wash each other for sleep,

the dead ones entering their gestures
and our discussion of love only as inflections

like trees bending in the wind.

PROTHALAMION

The love we've defined for ourselves
in privacy, in suffering,
keeps both of us lonely as a fist,
but does intimacy mean a happy ending?
I'm afraid of marriage.
Driving past them at night, the shadows
on a drawn curtain hide terrible lives:
a father stuck in a job, his daughter
opening her blouse to strangers.

And your hands, for example,
like a warm liquid on my face
don't evaporate as you take them away.
Nor are our betrayals silent,
although we listen only in passing.
We're learning how to walk unlit streets,
to see threats instead of trees,
the right answer to a teenager
opening his knife. The answer is yes.
Always we couldn't do otherwise.

HITTING FUNGOES

Hitting fungoes to a bunch
of kids who asked me
nicely, I'm afraid the hard
ball they gave me might
shatter the stained-glass
window of the church
across this abandoned lot.
I see it all now, in
the moment the ball leaves
my hand before it smacks
the bat: we scatter
in every possible direction,
but the pastor, sensing
a pervert, screams
to the cops to chase
the big one, and there
I am: trapped. I pull
my old Woodrow Wilson
Fellowship Letter out
of my worn suit pocket,
wave it wildly, but they
smell last night's sex
on my breath, condemn
me to jail for failure
to escape my terror of failure
itself. I swing without
thinking, the only way,
and the crack
is a heretic's hip-bone
ripped from its socket
on the rack. Not bad.
Not too deep, but a nice
arching loft. One kid,

who runs faster than the others,
makes a spectacular
diving catch and throws it back.

LETTERS FROM
AN INSTITUTION

The ward beds float like ghost ships
in the darkness, the nightlight
above my bed I pretend is a lighthouse
with a little man inside who wears
a sailor cap and tells good old stories
of the sea. The little man is me.
Perhaps I have a dog called Old Salt
who laps my hand and runs endlessly
down the circular stairs.
Perhaps he bites like sin.
I dream of ships smashing the reefs,
their bottoms gutting out,
the crews' disembodied voices screaming
Help us help us help somebody please
and there is no one there at all
not even me. I wake up nervous,
Old Salt gnawing my flesh. I wake up nervous,
canvas bedstraps cutting my groin.
The night nurse, making the rounds,
says I bellow in sleep like a foghorn.

◙

Nothing moves at night
except small animals
kept caged downstairs
for experiments, going
bullshit, and the Creole
janitor's broom whisking
closer by inches.
In the ward, we all

have room for errors and elbows
to flail at excitement.
We're right above the morgue;
the iceboxes make our floor
cold. The animals seem to know
when someone, bored with holding
on, gives out: they beat
their heads and teeth
against the chicken wire
doors, scream and claw.
The janitor also knows.
He props his heavy broom
against his belt, makes
a sign over himself
learned from a Cajun,
leaves us shaking
in our bedstraps
to drag the still
warm and nervous body
down from Isolation.

◙

I have a garden in my brain
shaped like a maze
I lose myself
in, it seems. They only look for me
sometimes. I don't like my dreams.

The nurses quarrel over where I am
hiding. I hear from inside
a bush. One is crisp

and cuts; one pinches. I'd like to push
them each somewhere.

They both think it's funny
here. The laughter sounds like diesels.
I won't come out because I'm lazy.
You start to like the needles.
You start to want to crazy.

DEATHWATCH

So close you're defenseless,
you inhale your father's last breath:
it sticks, did you steal it?,
this secret to begin yourself.
Here's how the secret works:
to fix you inside an immensity
that's merely a circular journey,
the trees leaning close
whispering Don't worry we'll tell you something,
the constant sun like punishment,
like the unspeakable loneliness of guilt.
In the otherwise actual world,
when you crawl away from your father
and can honor no thought but to flourish
wholly apart, people become
spectral and intimacies false.

Until a woman shows up
to rethread your obsession. Her touch shocks
like entering another person's dream—
but in her dream you discern
the chink in yourself you stepped out of
to get there, rubbing her gently as a weapon,
an oh-so-welcome temporary salvation
that would now seem like awakening

except you've never left your father.
He's getting colder,
his voice thin as an angel's,
although his tongue is stuck in death.
I need you so much, he says sweetly,
Come live in my mouth.

This is a poem for the dead

fathers: naked, you stand for their big faces,
mouths stuffed flat, eyes weighted, your miserable dick
sticking out like a nose. Dressed, you're more of
a mother making dinner: those old dirt bags,
the lungs, sway inside your chest like tits
in a housedress. Perhaps you're frying liver
that shrinks like your father getting older.
You still smell him breathing all over
your skin. He drank himself to death.

Now each woman you meet is a giant.
You'd crawl up their legs and never come down.
Even when you think you're big enough
to touch them, his voice flies from inside
your throat and "I love you" comes out
a drunk whimper. All you can do
is breathe louder. You're speaking
out of his mouth. Finally you admit
you know nothing about sex
and drown the urge slowly
like a fat bird in oil.

Still, those wings inside you.
At the hot stove all day you feel yourself
rising, the kids wrapping themselves
around your legs oh it's sexual
this nourishing food for the family
your father stumbling through the door
calling to you Honey I'm home.

A POSTHUMOUS POETICS

From embarrassment, I made statements.
My icons—tight caves and mouths—stuck together
briefly like dry lips, like a lover's insults.
The fact is they were ugly to all of us.
I said, How painstakingly personal!
Here are the words for this,
Relentless as insects! I was hysterical.

Every tone became artful,
the worst urges nuzzling like housepets
for someone to feel them, each real subject
demanding more real context for remarks.
Then abstractions insinuating their sharp edges,
asking to pry open privacies
alone in the bathroom at bedtime
then with strangers in elevators, at stop signs.
Even then, I knew you'd shun them,
because who would choose such intrusions?

I learned to love this isolation
as a woman who appears to listen.
All night I'd talk about my life
anticipating her dramatic relief,
believing her affectionate gestures filled in
what wasn't spoken. At those times
she seemed so genuine and friendly,
a voice from inside my own body
describing my shameless surrender
as our first kiss, perfect as gravity.

HOUSE

Nothing's unbroken in the house
that stands for happiness. You dance

to the music of its cracks, flexing
your muscles secretly like a priest,

wearing your body lightly as a robe
you don't need in this private place.

The closets welcome you with perfect
fits that kiss your skin with silk,

the attic's boarded like the cellar,
and the rooms, you discover,

are the same room. That's fine.
You adorn the one, dividing your mind

into four walls that bear the weight
they are meant to bear for all

who love you and would live here.

POEM AT THIRTY

The rich little kids across the street
twist their swings in knots. Near me,
on the porch, wasps jazz old nesting tunes
and don't get wild over human sweat.
This is the first summer of my middle life.
I ought to be content. The mindless harsh
process of history, with its diverse murders
and starvations, its whippings, humiliations,
child-tyrants, and beasts, I don't care for
or understand. Nor do I understand
restlessness that sometimes stops my sleep.

Waking, those mornings, is like being thrown from a train.
All you know comes to falling:
the body, in its witless crooning for solidity,
keeps heading for the ground.
There is no air, no sound, nothing
but dumb insistence of body weight
coming down, and there is no thought of love,
or passing time, or don't want to be alone.
Probably one hundred thousand impressions
wrinkle the brain in a moment like this,
but if you could think about it
you'd admit the world goes on in any case,
roars on, in fact, without you, on its endless iron track.

◙

But most mornings I ease awake:
also a falling,
but delicate as an agile wing
no one may touch with hands,
a transparent wing like a distant moan

arriving disembodied of pleasure or pain,
a wing that dissolves on the tongue,
a wing that has never flown.

Because I've awakened like this,
I think I could love myself quietly
and let the world go on.

So today I watched a pudgy neighbor
edge her lawn, and heard the small blade whine;
I saw her husband, the briefcase man,
whiz off in his Mercedes without a glance.
I believe I'm beginning to understand
that I don't know what such things mean:
stupid pain or pure tranquillity,
desire's dull ache or conquering the body,
the need to say we and be known to someone
or what I see in myself as I sit here alone.

The sun glares most mornings
like an executive's thick pinky diamond,
and slowly the dark backs off.
This is one reason this morning I awakened.

◙

No one can tell you how to be alone.
Some fine people I've known swirl to me
in airy forms like just so much hot dust.
They have all moved through in dreams.
A lover's smell, the gut laugh of a friend,
become hard to recall as a particular wind.

No one can tell you how to be alone.
Like the deep vacuum in sleep, nothing
holds you up or knocks you down, only
it doesn't end in waking but goes on and on.
The tangles of place, the floating in time,
you must accept gently like a favorite dream.

If you can't, and you don't, the mind
unlocks the mind. Madness, with his lewd grin,
always waits outside the window, always
wanting to come in. I've gone out before,
both to slit his throat and to kiss his hand.
No one can tell you how to be alone:

Watch tiny explosions as flowers break ground;
hear the children giggle, rapid and clean.
It's hard to care about ordinary things.
Doesn't pain expand from lack of change?
I can't grasp exactly the feelings of anyone.
No one can tell you how to be alone.

◘

At thirty the body begins to slow down.
Does that make for the quiet on this porch,
a chemical ability to relax and watch?
If a kid bounces her pelvis against a chain-link fence,
bounces so metal sings
and it seems she must be hurting herself,
how old must I get before I tell her to stop?

Right now, I let her do it.

She's so beautiful in her filthy T-shirt
and gym shorts, her hair swings with each clang,
and she can do no wrong.
I let her do it as background music
to storm clouds moving in like a dark army.
I let her do it as a fond wish for myself.
I feel the vibration of the fence
as a wasp feels voices on a pane of glass.
The song in it I can't make out.

This day, then, ends in rain
but almost everyone will live through it.
Tomorrow's thousands losing their loved ones
have not yet stepped into never being the same again.
Maybe the sun's first light will hit me
in those moments, but I'd gladly wake to feel it:
the dramatic opening of a day,
clean blood pumping from the heart.

WHEN I WAS CONCEIVED

It was 1945, and it was May.
White crocus bloomed in St. Louis.
The Germans gave in but the war shoved on,
and my father came home from work that evening
tired and washed his hands
not picturing the black-goggled men
with code names fashioning an atomic bomb.
Maybe he loved his wife that evening.
Maybe after eating she smoothed his jawline
in her palm as he stretched out
on the couch with his head in her lap
while Bob Hope spoofed Hirohito on the radio
and they both laughed. My father sold used cars
at the time, and didn't like it,
so if he complained maybe she held him
an extra moment in her arms,
the heat in the air pressing between them,
so they turned upstairs early that evening,
arm in arm, without saying anything.

CONSIDER A MOVE

The steady time of being unknown,
in solitude, without friends,
is not a steadiness that sustains.
I hear your voice waver on the phone:

Haven't talked to anyone for days.
I drive around. I sit in parking lots.
The voice zeroes through my ear, and waits.
What should I say? There are ways

to meet people you will want to love?
I know of none. You come out stronger
having gone through this? I no longer
believe that, if I once did. Consider a move,

a change, a job, a new place to live,
someplace you'd like to be. *That's not it,*
you say. Now time turns back. We almost touch.
Then what is? I ask. What is?

THE PURE LONELINESS

Late at night, when you're so lonely,
your shoulders curl toward the center of your body,
you call no one and you don't call out.

This is dignity. This is the pure loneliness
that made Christ think he was God.
This is why lunatics smile at their thoughts.

Even the best moment, as you slip
half-a-foot deep into someone you like,
sinks through the loneliness in it
to the loneliness that's not.

If you believe in Christ hanging on the cross,
his arms spread as if to embrace
the Father he calls who is somewhere else,

you still might hear your own voice
at your next great embrace, thinking
loneliness in another can't be touched,

like Christ's voice at death answering Himself.

WHERE I'LL BE GOOD

Wanting leads to worse than oddity.
The bones creak like bamboo in wind,
and strain toward a better life outside the body,
the life anything has that isn't human.

Feel the chair under you? What does it want?
Does lust bend it silly, like a rubber crutch?
Tell a tree about the silky clasp of cunt.
It won't shift an inch. It won't ache to touch.

Let me not cruise for teens in a red sports car,
or glare too long at what bubbles their clothes.
Let me never hustle file clerks in a bar.
Keep me from the beach when the hot wind blows.

If I must go mad, let it be dignified.
Lock me up where I'll feel like wood,
where wanting won't send me flopping outside,
where my bones will shut up, where I'll be good.

A Shape for It

Sometimes when time goes by,
I feel it bend.
The day becomes the same white room,
and the day won't end.

Its walls show no human scratch,
no useless wild attempt,
and echo no curse or cry,
but do not relent.

I wake amazed to be inside,
like an inmate slapped awake
while dreaming of an endless field
where the sun makes

festival of a girl's long yellow hair,
and she sways to gather
her dress as she waits,
and time seems clear as air.

A Changed Season

The tree has given its brief fruit
and the wind comes on with its weird caress.
Now, without stars, night seems limitless
like shadows of shadows over the earth.

She wanted to hold for one slim moment
leaves as they opened, the tree
unfolding its thin arms like a cripple
wheeled out for his afternoon sun.

But after any touch what stays on?
Wind, tree, or tongue, delicate and warm?
Better she curl in her own dark warmth
than try to go where they have gone.

GANGSTER DREAMS

Who made gangster dreams?
   The old moss on the brain.
Who calls to you upstairs?
   One in winter without a fire.
Who won't listen to you talk?
   I won't listen. You can't talk.
What's that face in the bedroom mirror?
   That's the gangster. He's the gangster.

What's trapped beneath the cellar?
   That's the gangster underwater.
Where's the house wrapped in fire?
   No one's house, with no one there.
What slim victim cries for air?
   That's the gangster. He's the gangster.
Who made gangster dreams?
   The old moss on the brain.

MEMORY

It's like watching an underwater show
through glass, where girls share
an air hose and ride huge fish.
My father drove us to see it
in the new '56 Buick, his gaudy Florida
shirt tattooed to his chest with sweat,
while we kids whaled on one another
in the back, read road signs, and whined
in concert until his backhand swung
blindly over the top of the seat,
clipping the unlucky one caught in its arc,
and that one would cry quietly to himself
while for five minutes the rest of us shut up.

Now, in this overlay of silences,
my father dead, me at my mother's house
for a brief visit, I recall our lives
seemed perfectly on the surface,
even if my sister had nervous attacks
and we were warned about strange men
who would try to pick us up.
Of course we are taken along by events
without grasping what's happening
until later when memory gives them shape
that may not encompass the facts.
But today I see my whole childhood
in the curves and flutterings of the girls
who had learned to smile while holding
their breath, and, though it must be only
a reflection on the glass, behind them
I see my father drowning in the tank.

In Winter

At four o'clock it's dark.
Today, looking out through dusk
at three gray women in stretch slacks
chatting in front of the post office,
their steps left and right and back
like some quick folk dance of kindness,
I remembered the winter we spent
crying in each other's laps.
What could you be thinking at this moment?
How lovely and strange the gangly spines
of trees against a thickening sky
as you drive from the library
humming off-key? Or are you smiling
at an idea met in a book
the way you smiled with your whole body
the first night we talked?
I was so sure my love of you was perfect,
and the light today
reminded me of the winter you drove home
each day in the dark at four o'clock
and would come into my study to kiss me
despite mistake after mistake after mistake.

ALL THE TIME

Intimate agonies should be wordless as birds,
small dull birds in dark scary woods,
but they don't care how they talk
or what beasts inside they become to break out.
The wind through those woods grows with them,
humming all night beneath hearing
like wire inside a building,
a wind pressing so gently
you'd think it understands.

It doesn't understand.
What you are and have been
forms the same answerless question,
the same relentless question bending you down
into a quiet resigned old man, while inside's
all pecking and screeching and mad flapping wings.
It happens all the time. Gravity in time
means flesh loosens and hangs, so the skeleton
emerging seems to say *this is what I am, it's what
I've always been.*
                    At least that is the illusion.

SEX

After the earth finally touches the sun,
and the long explosion stops suddenly
like a heart run down,
the world might seem white and quiet
to something that watches it in the sky at night,
so something might feel small,
and feel nearly human pain.

But it won't happen again:
the long nights wasted alone, what's done
in doorways in the dark by the young,
and what could have been for some.
Think of all the lovers and the friends!
Who does not gather his portion of them
to himself, at least in his mind?

Sex eased through everyone,
even when slipping into death
as into a beloved's skin,
and prying out again to find
the body slumped, muscles slack,
and bones begun their turn to dust.
Then no one minds when one lover
holds another, like an unloaded sack.

But the truth enters at the end of life.
It enters like oxygen into every cell
and the madness it feeds there in some
is only a lucid metaphor
for something long burned to nothing,
like a star.

How do you get under your desire?
How do you peel away each desire

like ponderous clothes, one at a time,
until what's underneath is known?
We knew genitals as small things
and we were ashamed they led us around,
even if the hill where we'd lie down
was the same hill the universe unfolded upon
all night, as we watched the stars,
when for once our breathing seemed to blend.

□

Each time, from that sweet pressure
of hands, or the great relief of the mouth,
a person can be led out of himself.
Isn't it lonely in the body?
The myth says we ooze about as spirits
until there's a body made to take us,
and only flesh is created by sex.
That's why we enter sex so relentlessly,
toward the pleasure that comes
when we push down far enough
to nudge the spirit rising to release,
and the pleasure is pleasure of pure spirit,
for a moment all together again.
So sex returns us to beginning, and we moan.

□

Pure sex becomes specific and concrete
in a caress of breast or slope of waist:
it flies through itself like light, it sails
on nothing like a wing, when someone's there
to be touched, when there's nothing wrong.

So the actual is touched in sex,
like a breast through cloth: the actual
rising plump and real, the mind
darting about it like a tongue.
This is where I wanted to be all along:
up in the world, in touch with myself . . .

Sex, invisible priestess of a good God,
I think without you I might just spin off.
I know there's no keeping you close,
as you flick by underneath a sentence
on a train, or transform the last thought
of an old nun, or withdraw for one moment alone.
Who tells you what to do or ties you down!

I'd give up the rest to suck your dark lips.
I'd give up the rest to fix you exact
in the universe, at the wildest edge
where there's no such thing as shape.

What a shame I am, if reaching the right person
in a dim room, sex holds itself apart
from us like an angel in an afterlife,
and, with the ideas no one has even dreamed,
it wails its odd music for pure mind.

◘

After there's nothing,
after the big blow-up of the whole shebang,
what voice from what throat
will tell me who I am? Each throat
on which I would have quietly set my lips

will be ripped like a cheap sleeve
or blown apart like the stopped-up
barrel of a gun. What was inside them
all the time I wanted always
to rest my mouth upon?

I thought most everything
stuck dartlike in the half-dome of my brain,
and hung there like fake stars in a planetarium.
It's true that things there changed into names,
that even the people I loved were a bunch of signs,
so I felt most often alone.
This is a way to stay alive and nothing to bemoan.
We know the first time we extend an arm:
the body reaches so far for so long.
We grow and love to grow, then stop, then lie down.

I wanted to bear inside me this tender outcome.
I wanted to know if it made sex happen:
does it show up surely in touch and talk?
does it leak from the mind, as heat from the skin?
I wanted my touching intelligent, like a beautiful song.

God
Hunger

NOT THE END OF THE WORLD

What flew down the chimney
into the cold wood stove
in my study? Wings
alive inside cast iron
gave the cold stove a soul
wilder than fire, in trouble.
I knocked the window screen out
with a hand-heel's thunk,
and dropped the shade over
the top half of the window,
and shut the study door,
and wadded the keyhole,
hoping whatever it was
would fly for the light,
the full, clean stream of light
like the sliding board from heaven
our guardian angels slid to earth on
in the *Little Catholic Messenger*
weekly magazine. I genuflected once,
but only to flick the stove-latch
and spring behind a bookcase
through a memory-flash
of church-darkness, incense smoke
mushrooming as the censer
clanks and swings back
toward the Living Host
in His golden cabinet.
A dull brown bird no bigger
than my fist hopped modestly
out, twisting its neck like a boxer
trying to shake off a flush punch.
And there on my rug, dazed,
heedless of the spotlight, it stayed,

and stayed, then settled down
as if to hatch an egg it was hallucinating.
So I scooped it into my two hands,
crazed heart in a feathered ounce,
and sat it outside on the dirt.

And there I left it.
It didn't even try its wings,
not one perfunctory flap,
but staggered a few rickety steps
before collapsing, puffing its tiny bulk.
I watched behind a window
other identical little dull birds
land within inches and chart circles
around it. Five of them,
cheeping, chased an inquiring cat.
Then all of them one by one—
by this time, a dozen—mounted its back
and fluttered jerkily like helicopters
trying to unbog a truck,
and, when that didn't work,
pecked it and pecked it,
a gust of flicks, to kill it
or rouse it I couldn't tell
until they all stepped back to wait.
It flapped once and fell forward
and rested its forehead on the ground.

I've never seen such weakness.
I thought to bring it back in
or call someone, but heard my voice
saying, "Birds die, we all die,"
the shock of being picked up again

would probably finish it,
so with this pronouncement
I tried to clear it from my mind
and return to the work I had waiting
that is most of what I can do
even if it changes nothing.

Do I need to say I was away
for all of a minute
before I went back to it?
But the bird was gone.
All the birds were gone,
and the circle they had made
now made a space so desolate
that for one moment I saw
the dead planet.

MY DREAM BY HENRY JAMES

In my dream by Henry James there is a sentence:
"Stay and comfort your sea companion
for a while," spoken by an aging man
to a young one as they dawdle on the terrace
of a beachfront hotel. The young man doesn't know
how to feel—which is often the problem
in James, which may have been the problem
with James, living, as he said, *in* the work
("this is the only thing"), shaping his late
concerti of almost inaudible ephemerae
on the emotional scale. By 1980,
when this dream came to me, the line spoken
takes on sexual overtones, especially since
as the aging man says it he earnestly presses
the young man's forearm, and in James
no exchange between people is simple,
but the young man turns without answering
to gaze over the balustrade at the ocean,
over the pastel textures of beach umbrellas
and scalloped dresses whose hems brush the sand,
without guessing the aging man's loneliness
and desire for him. He sees only monotony
as he watches waves coming in, and this odd
old man who shared his parents' table on the ship
seems the merest disturbance of the air,
a mayfly at such distance he does not quite hear.
Why should I talk to anyone? glides over his mind
like a cloud above a pond
that mirrors what passes over and does not remember.
But I remember this cloud and this pond
from a midweek picnic with my mother
when I was still too little for school
and we were alone together

darkened by shadows of pines
when with both hands she turned my face
toward the cloud captured in the water
and everything I felt in the world was love for her.

THIS IS WHY

He will never be given to wonder much
if he was the mouth for some cruel force
that said it. But if he were
(this will comfort her), less than one moment
out of millions had he meant it.

So many years and so many turns
they had swerved around the subject.
And he will swear for many more
the kitchen and everything in it vanished—

the oak table, their guests, the refrigerator door
he had been surely propped against—
all changed to rusted ironwork and ash
except in the center in her linen caftan:
she was not touched.

He remembers the silence before he spoke
and her nodding a little,
as if in the meat of this gray waste
here was the signal

for him to speak what they had long agreed,
what somewhere they had prepared together.
And this one moment in the desert of ash
stretches into forever.

They had been having a dinner party.
She had been lonely.
A friend asked her almost joking
if she had ever felt really crazy,

and when she started to unwind her answer
in long, lovely sentences like scarves within her
he saw that this was the way
they could no longer talk together.

And that is when he said it,
in front of the guests,
because he couldn't bear to hear her.
And this is why the guests have left
and she screams as he comes near her.

TV Room at the Children's Hospice

Red and green leather-helmeted
maniacally grinning motorcyclists
crash at all angles
on Lev Smith's pajama top

and when his chocolate ice cream
dumps like a mud slide down its front
he smiles, not maniacally, still nauseous
from chemotherapy and bald already.

Lev is six but sat still four hours
all afternoon with IVs in his arms,
his grandma tells everyone. Marcie
is nine and was born with no face.

One profile has been built in increments
with surgical plastic and skin grafts
and the other looks like fudge.
Tomorrow she's having an eye moved.

She finds a hand mirror in the toy box
and maybe for the minute I watch
she sees nothing she doesn't expect.
Ruth Borthnott's son, Richard,

cracked his second vertebra
at diving practice eight weeks ago,
and as Ruth describes getting the news
by telephone (shampoo suds plopped

all over the notepad she tried
to write on), she smiles like Lev Smith
at his ice cream, smiles also saying
Richard's on a breathing machine,

if he makes it he'll be quadriplegic,
she's there in intensive care every day
at dawn. The gameshow-shrill details
of a Hawaiian vacation for two

and surf teasing the ankles
of the couple on a moonlit beach walk
keep drawing her attention
away from our conversation.

I say it's amazing how life can change
from one second to the next,
and with no apparent disdain
for this dismal platitude

she nods yes, and yes again
at the gameshow's svelte assistant
petting a dinette set, and yes
to Lev Smith's grandma

who has appeared beside her
with microwaved popcorn
blooming like a huge
cauliflower from its tin.

THE GLADIATOR

*a tintinnabula apparently used
in Dionysiac rituals*
—*Erotic Art of Pompeii*

His cock is bigger than he is
and thickens out from his thighs
until it touches earth and curls
back to attack him with a mad dog's head:
jaws stretched, bared teeth, going for his throat.
Maybe the craftsman meant only to tell us
something simple through rough humor,
but the gladiator's countenance
radiates a madonna's calm
as the raised sword in his right hand
poises to chop down this-thing-grown-from-him
the instant its teeth will crush his neck,
and he just looks beyond it
at some miracle invisible to us.
The monstrosity, on the contrary,
seems gorged with anguish, bearing
all the anguish of this moment of no-time
it would kill everything to end.
Is this the punishment for being a man
who woke to see the evil he had become?
Or the defeat at the bottom of the self
exactly imagined, banished
by the sexual ritual of the bells?

MILK THE MOUSE

He'll pinch my pinky until the mouse starts squeaking.
The floor lamp casts a halo around his big stuffed chair.
Be strong Be tough! It is my father speaking.

I'm four or five. Was he already drinking?
With its tip and knuckle between his thumb and finger,
he'll pinch my pinky until the mouse starts squeaking

Stop, daddy, stop (it was more like screeching)
and kneels down before him on the hardwood floor.
Be strong Be tough! It is my father speaking.

What happened to him that he'd do such a thing?
It's only a game, he's doing me a favor
to pinch my pinky until the mouse starts squeaking

because the world will run over a weakling
and we must crush the mouse or be crushed later.
Be strong Be tough! It is my father speaking

to himself, of course, to the boy inside him weeping,
not to me. But how can I not go when he calls me over
to pinch my pinky until the mouse starts squeaking
Be strong Be tough? It is my father speaking.

MEETING CHEEVER

Iowa City, 1973

Above a half pizza and double gin,
his proffered hand trembled in the dark
as if, polished and slapped with cologne,
he had ridden a jackhammer from New York

that broke up everything inside
but politesse, which dangled like a hook:
informed you had just won a prize,
he said, "Ah yes, I loved your book."

And you, inconsolable bell-bottomed cliché
of wounded-by-the-world angry young poet
who became me as strangely as years become today,
replied, "The book's not published yet."

In a booth for four were mashed five
whose egos would have cramped the Astrodome.
One, thriving now, who still tries
to disguise his voice answering the phone

from decades of throwing bill collectors off,
whose wife told everyone her life was hell,
whose children had it rough,
was living by the week in a seedy motel.

He had killed a quart by noon
with a mountainous hard-boiled novelist
who thought "Chandler could write circles around *anyone*
with a piece of chalk in his ass."

Ungoaded, Cheever smiled at the figure
and said he'd love to see *that* manuscript.
Pinned between them, ankle to shoulder,
he looked like a sandwiched Siamese triplet

twice their age and half their size
but sharing one bloodstream—alcohol—
and one passion beyond themselves: stories
wild, precise, and beautiful.

My counterpart in the art of verse
was burbling his soda through a straw.
"Consciousness is a curse"
and "Coke-farts evoke sacred awe"

were his night's remarks, not addressed to us.
His poems were tiny nests of pain.
That Christmas he went to Panama in a VW bus
and no one ever saw him again.

And the hard-boiled novelist's new baby and wife,
then unconceived and not-yet-met,
that were said to have filled his life
with happiness and made him considerate,

died together in a crash.
Where was this future with its bloody claws?
Brilliant John Cheever is a handful of ash.
I would be done with what I was.

"Boy 'Carrying-In' Bottles in Glass Works"

West Virginia, 1911
Photograph by Lewis W. Hine

What makes his face heartbreaking
is that he wouldn't have it so—
just one of many boys working
amid splinters of glass that throw
such light they seem its only source
in this dusky photograph.
A random instant of the past.
And the brutal factory, of course,

is only one memory of brutality
on the world's infinite list.
The boy would be over eighty,
retired, unnoticed,
but surely he was stunted and is dead.
It's this look of his—
like a word almost said—
across an unchartable distance,

that shapes and bends
emotion toward him now,
though he wouldn't have it so.
He just looked into a lens
amid splinters of glass that throw
such light they seem its only source,
and rods and chutes that crisscross
like some malign, unnameable force.

WINTER DROUGHT

P. K. (1957–1977)

First you cut your wrists and throat,
then after they had sewn you up,
after three months of hospitals and talk,
after those who loved you cried themselves out
and their faces changed to sculptures of mistrust
in the early light, in the breakfast nook,
as you told them each day point-blank
how you felt about this life,
after they could no longer answer or look up,
you stole your father's car and drove it
to the bridge across the bay from Jamestown
where the police found it three days before
they found your body, bloated and frozen.
How could anyone so young want to die
so much? we asked, as if loneliness
tightens its death-grip gradually with age.
But we felt much older and lonelier ourselves
for a few days, until your terrible final image
began to fade and even your close friends
became again content enough
in that vast part of life
with families and earthly concerns
where your absence had never been noticed.
Such were the limits of friendship
you railed against, cursing its "ersatz intimacy"
one evening after a reading: in a crummy Cambridge bar,
with our uncomfortable group of ten
trapped in a half-moon booth,
you climbed onto the table and screamed,
and we heard you and could do nothing
but pick up broken glass and take you home.

Now it has been years.
You were nearly nothing to me—a friend
of a friend, a pushy kid who loved poetry,
one more young man alone in his distress—
but last week when I went out to where I sometimes walk,
across a field of chopped stalks yellowed and dried
by months of snowless winter,
you rose abruptly from the undercurrents of memory
dredged in a steel net, and I was there
where I never was, amid boat noise
and ocean stink, your corpse
twisting as if hurt
when the net broke the surface,
then riding toward me, motionless
pale blue against the water's black.
And I've seen you here every day since,
as if I were walking the beach
the moment you balance on the iced iron railing
and jump. Does such rage for pain
give immaculate clarity to things?
Like winter sunlight day after day
showing the field for what it is:
dust and splintered stalks
about to become dust?
Tell me what you want.

SPIDER PLANT

When I opened my eyes this morning,
the fact of its shooting out
long thin green runners on which miniatures
of the mother will sprout,
and that each of these offshoots
could in its own time repeat this,
terrified me. And something seemed awful
in the syllables of the word "Brenda,"
sounding inside me before they made a name,
then making a name of no one I've known.
I had been dreaming I was married to Patty
again. She kept coming on my tongue
and I knew if I put myself in
we'd have to stay together this time.
But I wanted to, and did, and as I did
the sadness and pleasure of our nine years together
washed through me as a river, yet
I knew this wasn't right, it couldn't
work, and though we were now enmeshed
forever, I began to rise from my body
making love with her on the bed and to hover
at a little distance over both of us.
That's when I awoke and saw the spider plant.

THROUGH A CRACK

That bird's odd chirp behind the fence
I thought the rasp of garden shears
I used as a boy to edge the lawn
late Saturday afternoons for years.

The neighborhood was quiet then.
The shades drawn tight against the heat.
The lawns all done, the bushes trimmed.
No sound but this escaped the street:

not Dougherty's incandescent, yattering TV,
not Galliano's shrieking fights,
not Quigley's muted .22
pinking rabbits from his bedroom by moonlight:

only the red, padded handles in my grip
and the stubby spring released and squeezed
and the *chik chik* of blue steel blades
as I inched along the border on my knees.

SEA WORMS

"Exotic Organisms Found in Pacific Ocean"
—*New York Times*

In sulfurous plumes of water
from vents in the bottom crust,
new life continuously forms
and thrives on what would kill us,

so maybe when you plunge
into your black, internal pit
something lovely and strange
will emerge from it.

Five-foot red-headed sea worms
that peek out of tubes they live in
don't look exactly in the photo
like blooming uncircumcision,

nor was the oceanographer kidding
describing that underworld scene
"like driving through a wheat field
in a submarine,"

but I tried to make it a joke
because I wanted you to laugh,
because I couldn't touch you,
because my love was useless,

because Chekhov was right—
"the soul of another lies in darkness"—
though I feel your cells call to mine
across the abyss of inches between us

when we lie in darkness together,
your luminous eyes wide open,
three miles deep in yourself
rooted in poison.

The Past

It shows up one summer in a greatcoat,
storms through the house confiscating,
says it must be paid and quickly,
says it must take everything.

Your children stare into their cornflakes,
your wife whispers only once to stop it,
because she loves you and she sees it
darken the room suddenly like a stain.

What did you do to deserve it,
ruining breakfast on a balmy day?
Kiss your loved ones. Night is coming.
There was no life without it anyway.

A BURGLARY

It was only of my studio at Yaddo,
a twenty-by-twenty cabin in the woods
whose walls are nearly all windows,
and all they got was a typewriter and stereo
(I say "they" though it may have been one burglar)
and something ludicrously cheap, like a stapler,
I didn't miss at first and now can't remember,
though I remember my not being able to find the thing weeks later
bringing the fact of the burglary back in a rush.
A discontinued Smith Corona, a decent stereo, maybe a stapler,
and a goose-neck desk lamp that belonged to Yaddo—
whereas next to the lamp on the desk, untouched,
were my bankbook and checkbook in full view.
The detective said, "This tells you they're pros."
(He said "they," too.) But maybe partly from seeing
so many paintings in open studios that summer,
the desktop with familiar objects removed
fixed into a still life: bankbook and checkbook
placed just so—blue analogous rectangles
rounding at the corners, miniature glazed deep pools,
and inside them whole schools of frantic ink numbers
suspended within such stolid form and color
they became flimsy and funny, a Duchamp joke, arbitrary,
the representation of what no one sees.
Also, the burglar(s) had slashed a window screen
into an inverted V that was sticking into the room like a tongue,
and had jimmied the window open
while the door was unlocked all along.
"Maybe this is actually a Happening," I said and laughed
with a sound like someone else clearing his throat.
I can still see the detective wearily scrutinizing my face
in the melting light of evening

a cross-draft seemed to wash in waves through the cabin
during the endless seconds before he asked, "What's that?"

All the Yaddo staff and most of the guests
offered regrets appropriate to a loss
which even to me did not sound great
inside the world's constant howl of misery—
plague and catastrophe pumped through TV,
the zillion sirens heard in a lifetime
each naming horror for someone.
When word of the burglary skittered through the dining room
(like a dropped glass goblet, in all directions),
a few guests dashed off to their studios to lock them,
and one woman, a conceptual artist
who had said my breathing while swimming
was "interesting" (she had crawled back and forth
along the pool's edge dunking her head
to listen "at ten-foot, half-minute intervals"),
dropped a fistful of dinner utensils
and cried, "My God, what if they stole *my* things!"
And a few, whose faces seemed to bob around me
like balloons, asked how I was feeling.

I said fine though I was not fine,
though not exactly because of the burglary.
I don't know how memory
shapes the present, and the present, memory;
but today, when I found these lines in my copy
of Hannah Arendt's *Thinking* (which I was reading then)
with my underscoring and stars in the margin—
"Solitude is being with oneself. Loneliness
is being with no one."—, I felt again

a desolation I had almost forgotten.
At Yaddo I could hear it whisper
like the voice of another person
mocking all I said outwardly calm or kind,
and, for months, teaching classes or at dinner with friends,
my mind might blank as if slammed
by a wave, and I'd struggle to pretend
I wasn't somersaulting underwater unable to breathe.
It now seems part of being crazy
not to ask for help or let anyone see,
but I felt happy alone in my studio
watching light striate in glyphs down the trees
and the leaves flash their silver undersides
when a gust bobbed the branch-tips
to nod *all right, all right* like tired old men.
With a symphony on the stereo blended in,
inside this cube of light and music and weightless shadow,
being alive felt like a gift. It didn't matter
where it came from or who or what was the giver.

So I was sure the burglary
was a retraction. What an old story:
Lapsed Catholic Still Sees Through Lens Of Religion:
if, for example, there's no actual Devil
he must be part of me. And so on.
To offset *Thinking* I was reading Greek myths
that say every god is both God and Devil;
that the gods are multiple and jealous;
that the impersonal, internal power balance on Olympus
determines our puny earthbound fates.
The puny burglary happened Saturday,
August fifteenth, during the Travers Stakes,
a festival day in Saratoga—not communal

(except for the race), but countless simultaneous days
running parallel on discrete economic levels
from high rollers in for the weekend to the locals.
The week previous I had met two blonde tipsy
doctors' wives slumming in a disco,
who invited me and about forty-four others
to a huge party the night of the Travers.
It was on the way to their party I first saw my studio
after the burglary: it looked hardly disturbed but dead,
the corpse of a natural, expected death,
as if the typewriter, lamp, and stereo
had been the soul of a life
that could be snuffed so easily and quick.
They still held to their places as shadows.
In the corner, a stack of books that had been next to a speaker
was knocked over, probably by accident,
and the loose-leaf notes crowning it scattered or flung.
The breeze through the gaping window and slashed screen
barely raised the papers' edges,
like hems of a white-gowned chorus
at the cue to take a breath and sing.
I figured I shouldn't touch anything.
The window was the one I always looked through.
I had never seen the trees through a slashed screen.
Had I never been there at exactly this time?
The light was different. Everything had changed.

The detective copied serial numbers from packing boxes
but said I could go ahead and kiss my stuff goodbye.
I sat at the desk a minute while he left in his Chevy.
After dinner I went to the party anyway,
following a map on a "Mine Shaft" cocktail napkin
scrawled over a cartoon barmaid in a mining helmet

with tiny ballpoint x's for the houses
so it looked like she was wearing a barbed-wire crown,
and found the street encircling the golf course,
and the house x-ed into the mining helmet's beam.
The husband, as it happened, wasn't a doctor
but a dentist, and it wasn't a huge party
but a buffet supper for twenty.
He jerked his wife into the kitchen
and wanted to know who exactly I might be,
when in fact it was her friend, the other woman,
with whom I had gone out to the parking lot
to have a drink in her Cadillac,
whose dashboard glowed with digital readouts
when she switched the ignition to play the tape deck,
whose front seat moved electronically,
she told me, to one hundred and one different positions,
then flicked her tongue across her teeth,
which, in that green glow, were exceedingly white.
"My husband likes this car," she said. "I hate it."
Now we were chatting on her friend's sun deck—
almost a hazard where a fairway doglegged—
elbow to elbow, with chinette plates.
Ten feet off, with golf-shirted cronies,
her husband—also a dentist—kept one eye on me
as if he were passing an unlit alley.
Whether from loneliness or perversity,
I stayed, and, after less than twenty minutes,
became, amazingly, just one of the party,
TV maybe creating a new human ability
to absorb discordant information instantly
and go on smiling as if the fact weren't happening.
The guests were all dentists, their wives, and hygienists;
all had long been curious about Yaddo

which stands like a Vatican in their midst.
In twos or threes, all twenty of them talked to me
("You're a poet? What do you *do*?"),
and someone's unemployed kid brother
who could have passed for a serial killer
recited his own personal poems to me
endlessly. I tilted my ear toward him and listened.
I thought this something I could do.
Maybe for this reason, if for no other,
everyone came to seem to feel pleasure
in my being there. I began enjoying myself, too,
until we heard, from the den this time,
the host dentist screaming at his wife:
"What the hell are you doing inviting to our *home*
some strange guy you meet in a bar?
To humiliate me? Or are you crazy?"
And everyone stopped their conversation
and looked in my direction. The voice in me
said *Stay. See what happens.* I knew where
it had come from. And I did stay there
a minute too long. In Mexico one time,
I was watching a movie in a neighborhood theater
when a knife blade slit the screen from behind.
I thought it must be an adolescent prank
until I heard over the soundtrack
someone not faking being stabbed and beaten.
The movie kept showing, shirts and hell shapes
flashing inside the shrieking black gash
while the audience exploded toward the exits.
(It turned out to be some dope lord's control tactics.)
Maybe my studio's slashed screen recalled it
without my knowing, because for that minute
I could still see all the guests looking at me

but on the deck with us was a vertical black cut.
Then it wasn't there. It wasn't. I put my drink down,
walked to the den, said I was very sorry, thanked them.
The two or three men who had followed me in
to make sure I was leaving and leaving quietly
and watched me back my car out of the driveway
looked like children at the window watching it rain.

I went back to The Mine Shaft then
and threw down shot after shot of bourbon
as a strobe underlighting the plastic multicolored dance floor
hammered the dancers into fragments.
I didn't want to die. I wanted to be nothing.
But last call came, overhead lights slapped on,
the parking lot demolition derby began,
wheels burning rubber and furious chromed engines,
and the women who were still with friends
hooked arms to step briskly through dog packs of men
screaming furious invitations into their faces.
I drove back to my studio shouting nonsense,
snapped on the bare bulb on the ceiling,
and sat at my desk drinking six-packs watching
my redoubled reflections in fourteen black windows
until the dawn erased the faintest ones
and minute by minute they all faded to nothing.
At one point that night I talked to each in sequence,
spitting I don't know what insults, and they
talked back, came to life, told me off,
fourteen, fourteen hundred at once, until I found myself
speed-walking a circle around the room.
Anybody going by would have thought I was crazy,
and I guess I *was* crazy, but I remember
I was trying to see myself as a stranger

by becoming person after person
I had talked to that day.

I had only a few more weeks at Yaddo.
Someone loaned me a typewriter. The lamp was replaced
by a silver architect's model that clamped to the desk.
Nobody had an extra stereo.
Before I could make myself sit in the studio
during the daylight for an hour or two,
the dentist's wife came to see me in her Cadillac,
which looked even more wacky in daytime
parking next to the used Subarus and Toyotas
of painters and composers. One by one,
I pulled the fourteen brittle yellow shades
down over the windows, and the light
turned the color of peach-meat.
She told me the host had stormed out
after I left the party, they didn't know if he was after me,
but he didn't come back all night
and he and her friend were getting a divorce.
I couldn't guess why she had come to tell me this.
What could I do about it? And we sat there
with not another word to say to each other,
me at the desk, her in the armchair.
So when she said finally,
"I really came to apologize for the party,"
I didn't reply: "Apologize? It was my fault."
Or: "*You* didn't do anything wrong."
Or: "That's not necessary" or "How kind."
But: "I really don't want to be part of all this,"
before it had been in my mind.
"Of course. Why would you?" she said quickly,
softly, looking down, looking away.

But both of us knew here was no tragedy.
Neither of us could ever love the other.
Nothing called up our courage or honor.
Yet something began filling the room like water—
rust-color, thick as the merger of the slow orange light
and silence between us, or maybe it was the light
and silence becoming one thing apart from us,
apart from anyone or anything human.
I can't imagine what she felt except discomfort
and the generosity to part without meanness.
Her eyes looked past me scanning the room
and the sudden pleasure on her face must have come from
her recalling what I had mentioned at the party
and thinking it a way to push through our embarrassment:
"Well, Michael," she said cheerily, "tell me about the burglary."
I couldn't tell her much, but I wanted to.

A SPLINTER

A twinge forgotten by the body
among its million daily nerve-firings;
and a moment uncolored by consciousness,

the thick paperback splayed
on your lap at the place you stopped
who knows what phantom universe

after Anna Karenina,
poisoned by poison-love,
throws herself under the iron horse

and you had been taken into her thinking
Where am I? What am I doing? Why?
She wanted to rise and draw back

but something enormous and implacable
struck her head and dragged her along.
"Oh Lord, forgive me all my sins!" she

screams as the tall wheels
crush and split her silk dress,
ravenous flesh, and delicate skeleton.

In the station on the platform
you turned away
from her pain finally done

and laid the book down.
The mind, released then,
began to fill with its native emptiness,

idle thoughts darting
like translucent minnows in a clear shallow.
You lifted your hand to gaze

with wonder at the palm and fingers
as if they weren't your own,
as you have since childhood

how many times, and noticed
a splinter under a fingertip
and began digging through the skin for it

with fingernails then a nailfile
then a cuticle scissors until you bled
and it slid out, impaled softwood,

moist, black as an eyelash,
and you came back to your own life
crying not for yourself.

ONE

. . . six million dead,
a million of them children.

A ten-year-old
in a crinoline, her neck
inclined like a bather
by Degas, her washed black
hair spilling forward
over her crown and forehead
because the sheep shears
has begun to clip at her nape,
and for this split second
the first puffball of hair
balances on the unearthly
blue-white knuckles of the hand
about to drive these clippers
up her skull. This image
from nowhere particular
(photos or movies or newspaper
stories) caught in a gauze
of grayness and cold—
did it ever really happen to
this little girl, the wispy hollow
at the base of *her* skull
shocked by freezing stainless steel?
I have to think
to follow from the hand
up the emblazoned sleeve,
to see the ovens in the background,
to imagine what I can't
imagine but can only name:
her mother's anguish,
her father's nightmare terror
ensnarled with their fear

for themselves and for each other—
has she lost them already
or are they watching her?
There must have been soldiers
whose Nazi blinders
were seared through by the horror,
but all I see of them
in this split second
are blue-white knuckles
working an implement
used on animals
on this little girl
who dressed last night for a party,
and now, too confused to cry,
stands somewhere amid
barbed wire and mud
her head being shaved.

PORTRAIT OF A LADY

*...because she was in that state
so many young girls go through — a
state of sexual obsession that can
be like a sort of trance.*
— Doris Lessing

Was it only the new old chemical stirrings
that made her shoplift purple corduroys
and squeeze into them out of her mother's hearing
to discover what noises could come from boys?

"Like sleepwalking on stilts," she laughed years later
about the cheap spiked heels wobbling under her feet.
The lip-smacks and wolf whistles she remembered
as fainter than the slamming of her own heartbeat

when she appeared to herself in the overlit mirror
that Saturday afternoon in the shopping mall john.
All the stoned girls quit primping and stared.
And time stopped. Then one stuck out her tongue.

Our lady flipped that little whiffet the finger
and spent her strength to yank open the door
and promenade bravely past Sears and What-A-Burger
down the white-hot, phosphorescent corridor

to draw a boy to her who would answer her anger.
Of course what she got was bruises from their pawing,
fast rides, dumb jokes, and thorough ignorance of her.
But what could she do when need came gnawing?

One day she saw the answer playing Space Invaders.
His fury charged his body like a thick, hot wire.
And she'd meet him there and do anything he told her,
until for no reason he didn't show up anymore.

This is the time she marked as her awakening:
the slow hours picking through the heart's rubble
and finding only shards of incomprehensible pain.
Then *she* broke hearts, got a teacher in trouble,

and never gave herself wholly to anyone again.
But cruelty was a drug she needed less with age.
She lived calmly with a husband and children
and her body locked around her like a cage.

FIRST EXERCISE

I was swimming
because I wanted to get skinny,
having passed the age of thirty
when the body begins its gradual revenge
for all those days of inattention
it secretly begrudged all along.
So I was finally paying it my full attention,
pulling it back and forth
across the pool's width at the baby end;
standing after each lap to wait for breath
and study the excellent rhythms of the swimmers
in the roped lanes of the Olympic pool adjoining,
as the light through high, leaded windows
broke into diamonds off their wakes;
nodding in turn to my companions at this end:
two impossibly vigorous, white-capped old men
and a dark woman in a black spandex suit
that fit her like skin. I've always hated swimming
for impeccable reasons, especially since
I'm nearly blind without my contact lenses
and I didn't understand the new goggles
I bought for my new regimen did not mean
I could keep my lenses in and see new things;
so from one of my fancy underwater racing turns
I came up without them,
and touched my eyes, and looked, and felt
a rush of panic into my chest,
the shock when someone says
there's been a terrible accident
and you don't know who or what.
Of course, after a second, I thought
"It's only your contact lenses,"
but I dived for them anyway again and again,

trying to hold myself under to pet the tile
with my palms, and later, as I walked home,
the world a blur of dull color run together,
I thought of my friend diving at dusk
in that mountain lake for his daughter
and what came to him when his hands
sank into the cold mud at the bottom.

THE DITCH

In the ditch, half-ton sections of cast-iron molds
hand-greased at the seams with pale petroleum waste
and screw-clamped into five-hundred-gallon cylinders
drummed with rubber-headed sledges inside and out
to settle tight the wet concrete
that, dried and caulked, became Monarch Septic Tanks;
and, across the ditch, my high school football coach,
Don Compo, spunky pug of a man,
bronze and bald, all biceps and pecs,
raging at some "attitude" of mine
he snipped from our argument about Vietnam—
I mean *raging,* scarlet, veins bulging from his neck,
he looked like a hard-on stalking back and forth—
but I had started college, this was a summer job,
I no longer had to take his self-righteous, hectoring shit,
so I was chuckling merrily, saying he was ludicrous,
and he was calling me "College Man Ryan"
and, with his steel-toed workboot, kicking dirt
that clattered against the molds and puffed up between us.

It's probably not like this anymore, but every coach
in my hometown was a lunatic. Each had different quirks
we mimicked, beloved bromides whose parodies we intoned,
but they all conducted practice like boot camp,
the same tirades and abuse, no matter the sport,
the next game the next battle in a neverending war.
Ex-paratroopers and -frogmen, at least three
finally convicted child molesters, genuine sadists
fixated on the Commie menace and our American softness
that was personally bringing the country to the brink of collapse—
in this company, Don Compo didn't even seem crazy.
He had never touched any of us;
his violence was verbal, which we were used to,
having gotten it from our fathers

and given it back to our brothers and one another
since we had been old enough to button our own pants.
Any minute—no guessing what might trigger it—
he could be butting your face mask and barking up your nostrils,
but generally he favored an unruffled, moralistic carping,
in which I, happy to spot phoniness,
saw pride and bitterness masquerading as teaching.
In the locker room, I'd sit where I could roll my eyeballs
as he droned, but, across the ditch,
he wasn't lecturing, but fuming, flaring
as I had never seen in four years of football,
and it scared and thrilled me to defy him and mock him
when he couldn't make me handwash jockstraps after practice
or do pushups on my fingertips in a mud puddle.

But it was myself I was taunting. I could see my retorts
snowballing toward his threat to leap the ditch
and beat me to a puddle of piss ("you craphead,
you wiseass"), and my unspading a shovel from a dirt pile
and grasping its balance deliberately down the handle
and inviting him to try it.
Had he come I would have hit him.
There's no question about that.
For a moment, it ripped through our bewilderment,
which then closed over again
like the ocean
if an immense cast-iron mold were dropped in.
I was fired when the boss broke the tableau.
"The rest of you," he said, "have work to do,"
and, grabbing a hammer and chisel, Don Compo
mounted the mold between us in the ditch
and with one short punch split it down the seam.

SMOKE

There was a woman whose husband had died,
the mother of one of my sister's friends,
we took her to lunch when a few weeks
had gone by, she sat in the back
between my sister and me the whole way there
dress up to her thighs, leg flush against mine,
chatting to my parents in the front seat
about her plans to move away, and when I
held the car door for her, she slid out slowly,
one leg at a time, so I'd see the plump silk
underneath, then grazed me so lightly
as she stood up I was never sure
if she had touched me or not.

And what of it?
What of a secret that takes you, to which
you give yourself, that stays with you,
to which you can return as to a pleasure
in a drawer, until some remote
future afternoon when it's there again
after not being with you for such a long time
you can't remember when it was forgotten?
When I lay down for a nap today,
the light softened
as if the windows were being smeared with Vaseline
and a fantasy began that I like
but I thought no, I always have this,
what about another, one I used to have,
and there was the woman whose husband had died
and my life in the world seemed made of smoke.

HOUSEFLIES

It's not them that make me crazy
but they seem the essence of madness,
ramming the window headfirst
yet clicking like fingernails on the glass.

In this disproportionate quiet,
with old newspapers rolled in my fist,
I wait one by one when they light
for their hairspring legs to relax,

which means their insect attention
has shifted wrongly
from the danger of death,
and they are probably lucky

they don't get a chance to reflect
on how they acquired bad instinct
before my bludgeon of published disasters
turns them each to a pinch of smash.

But they must have a nest in the woodwork.
When the sun makes my window hot,
they are always there pressing on it,
the same eight thick black knots.

LARKINESQUE

Reading in the paper a summary
of a five-year psychological study
that shows those perceived as most beautiful
are treated differently,

I think *they could have just asked me,*
remembering a kind of pudgy kid
and late puberty, the bloody noses
and wisecracks because I wore glasses,

though we all know by now how awful it is
for the busty starlet no one takes seriously,
the loveliest women I've lunched with
lamenting the opacity of the body,

they can never trust a man's interest
even when he seems not just out for sex
(eyes focus on me above rim of wineglass),
and who *would* want to live like this?

And what does beauty do to a man?—
Don Juan, Casanova, Lord Byron—
those fiery eyes and steel jawlines
can front a furnace of self-loathing,

all those breathless women rushing to him
while hubby's at the office or ball game,
primed to be consumed by his beauty
while he stands next to it, watching.

So maybe the looks we're dealt are best.
It's only common sense that happiness
depends on some bearable deprivation
or defect, and who knows what conflicts

great beauty could have caused,
what cruelties one might have suffered
from those now friends, what unmanageable
possibilities smiling at every small turn?

So if I get up to draw a tumbler
of ordinary tap water and think *what if this were
nectar dripping from delicious burning fingers,*
will all I've missed knock me senseless?

No. Of course not. It won't.

THE CROWN OF FROGS

In Bertolucci's *1900*, half brothers—
the son and bastard son of an estate owner—
are born in the same hour and grow up
as twins, learning as they grow older
the difference between them, the one
being groomed with education for power,
while the other is worked all day like an animal
then left on his own to roam the farm.

They realize that they have changed,
changed from mirrors to shadows of each other,
when the rich son finds the poor one
snatching frogs from a stream and stringing them
around the crown of his hat onto a circular wire
that twangs apart each time he flicks
the hook and eyelet at his temple
like the trigger of a homemade gun.

No one hears the sound but him.
It's muffled on the soundtrack under their soprano Italian
and the crystalline, shade-dappled, ankle-deep water
gurgling over the rocks. The crown of frogs
above his Huck Finn face fills the screen
as he talks, as he mocks rich-boy clumsiness,
then cuffs the water and jams another frog onto the wire
without breaking the flow of his abuse,

he has become so expert practicing on himself
in the hours he has been given to waste.
The frogs are his bitterness incarnate, his brain
turned inside out, squirming, bleeding
in trickles where the wire threads the gills,

one leg or two or ten abruptly straightened
as if a shock circled the wire
down into these pale underbellies of despair

bloating and releasing the air
in great sighs, in hopeless torpor.
Twenty years later a Fascist monster
rapes another little boy in a cellar
then swings him by his heels into a wall
in a scene that to me is film's most sickening:
knickers tangle at the ankles
as offscreen his head thuds, and thuds again,

and, though who can bear it?, thuds a final time
before the legs go white and lifeless.
Neither half brother becomes that murderer,
but I walked from the theater stunned
into a forgotten Florida afternoon
with my dad's new boss's son
who was exactly my age, the age
of the children in the film, eight or nine.

For weeks beforehand I had been warned
to be nice to him. While our parents
lounged on the patio with Windex-blue drinks,
he took me out beyond the fence
of his vast backyard to his secret place
where he had strung a wire clothesline
between two palmettos, and, in the marsh grass
underneath, had stashed bamboo poles with

tiny wire nooses attached to their tips.
"These are the prisoners," he announced,

and from the marsh grass he produced
a valentine candy-box crisscrossed with rubberbands
and icepick holes in each chamber of the heart.
"And that's the graveyard," pointing to a plot of
turned earth all slimy and wet.
"Do you want to see one hung?"

I said *what hung* but he couldn't hear me then.
His eyes glazed as he probed two fingers into the box
and brought to within an inch of my nose
a buttery, brown, tiger-striped toad
squeezed so tightly in his fist
I was afraid its head would pop out like a cork.
Then he looped it in a noose
and cast it over the clothesline.

"Watch it *piss!*" he screeched, and, as the toad
twisted and swung, the needle-stream
cut the air into patterns of contorted diamonds,
and he wheezed "Hee . . . hee . . . hee . . ."
unable to breathe until the toad
choked and swayed to rest and hung
plumb and quiet for one endless minute.
Then he buried it and dug some others up.

The toad instead of himself: it now seems obvious.
His unspeakable language now seems obvious.
Even then I knew I had been a witness to madness,
and, after I talked him back to the house,
swearing to share his secret with no one else,
my mother held out her hand to me
to step back up onto the patio
that felt like an ice floe on a sea of oil.

But life's not like the movies.
That afternoon nothing changed dramatically.
We weren't swept into a terrible current of history.
Should the sky have rained fire and the earth
opened in outrage? We all just sat there
on our loungers until evening—two silent little boys,
one crazy, and four adults: soft, pale people
in black elastic knee socks and plaid Bermuda shorts.

PASSION

Chilly early Saturday, my study
its usual chaos: a cluster of half-digested paperbacks
around the stuffed chair and floor lamp
thinning to the rug's periphery
like a molecule's probability graph;
stacks of drafts for this or that poem
or essay, flashes temporarily shaped
into one of a trillion possible embodiments,
encrusted now before a wicker wastebasket
erupting months of slamdunked crumpled
legal sheets and loose-leaf; and me—
happy after waking next to you—
diffused through this minuscule universe,
a larger but less cohesive bit of matter
than the poster of the pre-Columbian
fertility goddess staring at no one
from above my desk. I'm writing this,
for instance, because Maria Rodriguez
beams from the pile of old Sunday *Times*
I twist into knots for kindling
to get my wood stove going in the morning.
She's hugging the man she married
at San Quentin the moment the photo
was taken, where marriages are performed
in the hospitality room the first Tuesday
every month, where this month (June 1982)
there were eleven. For a few minutes
I sit crosslegged before the stove's mouth
and try to ride with her on the free bus
for convicts' families from Los Angeles—
squabbling toddlers, rap music pumping
from a boom box, her heels and dress tucked
in an overnight case on the overhead rack

with the pearl eyeshadow she'll redo one last time
in the video-scanned hospitality room
before her man appears behind the glass partition
and floats like that, ghostly, in her mind
as she changes back afterward into her everyday clothes
for the night ride home. Maria Rodriguez
says her friends tell her she's crazy,
and her family, forget it, none of them
would come. Statistics prove these marriages
collapse after the prisoner's released,
but it's not for then she's marrying.
It's for this passion
she had only dreamed, that she thought
happened only in movies and never believed
could be real. I believe it's real.
I remember us trying to talk about it
the day the article was published.
Passio, "suffering; Christ's scourging
and crucifixion," the Latin
from the Indo-European root for *harm*
from which also comes Greek for *destruction.*
As you read me the etymology, it melted
easily into the sacred music of Scarlatti
and aroma of coffee and bacon
that swell our home on Sunday mornings
when love seems uncomplicated and kind.
I don't remember what I said or did
the rest of that day—worked in here probably,
read the paper, watched baseball on TV—
but this morning, knotting this page for the fire,
I thought of keeping it. I thought
of clipping the photo of Maria Rodriguez
and tacking it in here so she would tell me

if I forget what passion means.
I thought of it, then jammed it
into the stove and gave it to the flames.

Pedestrian Pastoral

It's nothing to a squirrel
to vault ten times its pulsing length
and come down running on a branch
thin as a popsicle,

and much less to a groundhog
flattened by a tire
to hold one perfect paw in air
as if summoning a partner,

and this unexpectedly gorgeous
shaggy white cow, inexplicably
alone in a pasture—
what is it to her this December

if at her black nose breath-puffs
vanish and appear like a Don't Walk
warning blinker? But I do walk
happily in this mild Virginia winter

unable to feel absolutely sure
I won't be here forever
almost like this, a pure observer,
for once oblivious

to the spurs of ego and desire
that—whatever death is
or is not—could be paradise
to finally do without.

MOONLIGHT

It silvers the lawn,
its off-white wash tingeing
these hours alone,
frozen dewdropped grassblades
an army of sparklers
I would love like Walt Whitman
to insinuate myself among,
drawing them out about home
before I write their letters for them
and dress the gangrenous wounds
they will soon die from,
petting the feverish ones,
kissing one or two of them
open-mouthed, long, and lingering,
my gift-satchel emptied,
my heart broken.
If you were beside me, you'd say,
"It looks like snow, only invisible,"
and the world moonlight makes,
in which even roof-tin
glints like platinum, could seem
a distillation of joyous thought,
all clarity and outline,
the great winter-stripped maple
you married me under in summer
flaring its black skeleton against the sky
as I walk straight for it
praying for no more words between us
that are killing everything.

FIRE

I think of myself as dust of bones
mornings when I awake
to find the fine white ash
lining the bottom of my box stove.
Each night I slide in
logs thicker than the circle
of my thigh, and watch them all
blaze for a while,
because I'm about to sleep
and know that what I'll see encircles me
as if I were having no dream
but it is having me.
With the fire, in the darkened room,
my life begins not to be my own,
a pulse of watery blue transparencies
inside the jagged flames
that die and flare again,
while on the underside begin
orange coals that should seem
so cool and delicious on the tongue,
and all of it nothing by morning.

TOURISTS ON PAROS

If I die or something happens to us
and a stray breeze the length of the house
takes you alone back to that June on Paros
when we wrote every morning in a whitewashed room
then lay naked in the sun all afternoon
and came back at dusk famished for each other
and talked away the night in a taverna by the water—
I hope the memory gives you nothing but pleasure.

But if you also suddenly feel the loss
snap open beneath like a well covered with grass,
remember our stumbling in T-shirts and shorts
onto that funeral party in the café at breakfast:
not the widow, barely sixteen, in harsh wool cloth,
nor the grief that filled the air and seemed boundless,

but the brawny, red-haired Orthodox priest
whose shaggy orange beard over his black-smocked chest
was like an explosion from a dark doorway
of a wild, high-pitched laugh.

CROSSROADS INN

Sitting on a rock
as someone might have done
two hundred years ago
next to this fire-brick tavern,

I can feel the Virginia hills
surge up to my feet.
They are like waves stopped still.
In the declivities between,

an asphalt strip of road
curls and disappears,
and a vulture is overhead
climbing, pumping the air

with earnest, floppy strokes
beneath black hawks that ride
the high currents like smoke.
And something turns in my mind

when I follow the road below
as far as I can see:
two hundred years ago,
needing rest and company,

a drover walking livestock
to a nearby river port
stopped here overnight
and in the evening sat on this rock

thinking *What will be here
two hundred years from now*
and the surging hills answered
Nothing that you know.

A POSTCARD FROM ITALY

I can't tell you how beautiful
is the flowering of water
in this park in Florence
on Sunday afternoon in October,
but a rusty cluster of nozzles
fires water-jets toward the sun
in arcs that land as a star-shape
on a little circular pond
defined by white stones
and diffused by white swans.
And everyone stopping
different trouble in different lives
may share for a while
this particular calm—
this patter of water, gray shade
of evergreens, and always amazing
slow gliding of the swans.
I know the photos of teenagers
taking one another's pictures
mugging in the crotch
of an ancient, gnarled cedar
may be found years from now in a shoebox
by someone to whom they mean nothing,
and the innocence of children
whipping around the pond
in rented push-pedal carts
might become some greedy adult obsession,
but this old woman in black
who had been walking here
with her hands clasped behind her neck
like a prisoner
just threw back her head to stretch
her palms toward the sun,
and I wish somehow you could see her.

STONE PAPERWEIGHT

I was napping as usual
between our dinner and your bedtime
so I would be alert working
in the timeless hours before dawn

in which I become almost bodiless
because the world has black gloves on
its touching agonies and beauties
and leaves me happily alone—

when you broke into my dream
before I woke with your lying down
freshly naked against me
in flesh cool as the stone

I was dreaming you found at a shoreline,
worn flawless by water and sand,
and gave me to weight my papers
against the disturbing wind.

GOD HUNGER

When the immutable accidents of birth—
parentage, hometown, all the rest—
no longer anchor this fiction of the self
and its incessant *I me mine,*

then words won't be like nerves in a stump
crackling with messages that end up nowhere,
and I'll put on the wind like a gown of light linen
and go be a king in a field of weeds.

TANGLEWOOD

We were trying to talk about love,
and blank pain that stays blank
until music makes a shape for it,
so to know it, so to feel it out,
when you said, "Look, we've joined a swarm!"—
we had become another couple among hundreds
converging to get in, hand in hand, blankets
under arms, wine bottles swinging by the necks
like pendulums of old clocks. You said,
"Let's try not to talk until the music's over,"

but when it began, and the light was almost gone,
someone showed us how she loved a man
the way her back inclined sitting next to him,
the way her hand traveled his back and neck
as if there were no limits to her touch,
as if there had been no demarcations drawn
and she believed she had found the one
from whom to take essential sustenance
and felt no need to seek it anywhere else.
You said, "I've never felt that way myself."

And then, "Maybe it can happen for
only a few moments in a life."
All the other couples near our blanket
had made other arrangements, upright
in lawn chairs or scattered on the grass.
One man curled up with his back to his wife,
his head pillowed on the inside of his wrist,
while she sat hugging her knees to her chest
as if they had argued to exhaustion,
and just switched off the light.

But soon you were drawn inside the music.
The air suffused with music and you breathed it.
Darkness thickened so those surrounding
became black cutouts melded or apart.
You lay back, eyes wide, listening hard,
to watch the crossing of the music and the stars,
to feel yourself nothing but some chance meeting
of endless space and endless inwardness,
to float if only for a minute with the music
over touches useless, and tender, and electric.

SWITCHBLADE

Most of the past is lost,
and I'm glad mine has vanished
into blackness or space or whatever nowhere
what we feel and do goes,
but there were a few cool Sunday afternoons
when my father wasn't sick with hangover
and the air in the house wasn't foul with anger
and the best china had been cleared after the week's best meal
so he could place on the table his violins
to polish with their special cloth and oil.
Three violins he'd arrange
side by side in their velvet-lined cases
with enough room between for the lids to lie open.
They looked like children in coffins,
three infant sisters whose hearts had stopped for no reason,
but after he rubbed up their scrolls and waists
along the lines of the grain to the highest sheen,
they took on the knowing postures of women in silk gowns
in magazine ads for new cars and ocean voyages,
and, as if a violin were a car in storage
that needed a spin around the block every so often,
for fifteen minutes he'd play each one—
though not until each horsehair bow was precisely tightened,
and coated with rosin, and we had undergone an eon of tuning.
When he played, no one was allowed to speak to him.
He seemed to see something drastic across the room
or feel it through his handkerchief padding the chin board.
So we'd hop in front of him waving or making pig noses
the way kids do to guards at Buckingham Palace,
and after he had finished playing and had returned to himself,
he'd softly curse the idiocy of his children
beneath my mother's voice yelling to him from the kitchen
That was beautiful, Paul, play it again.

He never did, and I always hoped he wouldn't,
because the whole time I was waiting for his switchblade
to appear, and the new stories he'd tell me
for the scar thin as a seam
up the white underside of his forearm,
for the chunks of proud flesh on his back and belly,
scarlet souvenirs of East St. Louis dance halls in the Twenties,
cornered in men's rooms, ganged in blind alleys,
always slashing out alone with this knife.
First the violins had to be snug again
inside their black cases
for who knew how many more months or years or lifetimes;
then he had to pretend to have forgotten
why I was sitting there wide-eyed across from him
long after my sister and brother had gone off with friends.
Every time, as if only an afterthought,
he'd sneak into his pocket and ease the switchblade
onto the bare table between us,
its thumb-button jutting from the pearl-and-silver plating
like the eye of some sleek prehistoric fish.
I must have known it wouldn't come to life
and slither toward me by itself,
but when he'd finally nod to me to take it
its touch was still warm with his body heat
and I could feel the blade inside aching
to flash open with the terrible click
that sounds now like just a *tsk* of disappointment,
it has become so sweet and quiet.

New
Poems

A Two-Year-Old Girl
in a Restaurant

Your delight, which is contagious,
has been occasioned by
the twinkling point of a steak knife
about to liquify your eye,

so when your father swats it
from your prehensile fist
you squinch your blooming face
tight as a blastocyst

as if all the world's pain
had conceived inside your skull
and you, the prima diva
of the coloratura wail,

go deep into your soul
to sing how such pain feels,
and we remember well
and smile or do not smile.

OUTSIDE

The dead thing mashed into the street
the crows are squabbling over isn't
her, nor are their raucous squawks
the quiet cawing from her throat
those final hours she couldn't speak.
But the racket irks him.
It seems a cruel intrusion into grief
so mute it will never be expressed
no matter how loud or long the wailing
he might do. Nor could there be a word
that won't debase it, no matter
how kind or who it comes from.
She knew how much he loved her.
That must be his consolation
when he must talk to buy necessities.
Every place will be a place without her.
What people will see when they see him
pushing a shopping cart or fetching mail
is just a neatly dressed polite old man.

THE MUSIC HOUSE

Nobody's home in the music house.
It's dark tonight. I've never seen it dark.
It's filled with light at night,
cars parked in front up and down the street,
the picture window like a movie screen
of music: piano, oboe, cello, violin;
duos, trios, string quartets—from night to night
the place seems bursting.
I see the players in suits or black sheaths.
They're all Japanese. I want to go in
in my jogging shorts and ask them,
"May I just stand in back and listen?"
I run-in-place a little while outside instead.
The living room's furnished with folding chairs
and music stands. There's always music in it.
That's the furniture, I guess. A music teacher
lives here. After school and weekends, minivans
drop off children toting hard-black-cased instruments.
They're all so earnest and determined, especially the older ones.
Some play well, too, but most are awful.
They squeak something awful, butchering
the melody line with their weak fingering.
The music teacher stands over them.
She makes them play the practice piece all the way through,
again, then again. How can she bear to be near it?
I can't see her face from the street.
She stands with her back to the window.
At night I don't see her either, or don't know if I do.
I don't know which woman she is.
Maybe I would if I could see differently, or if I were Japanese.
Night's when she must get what she needs—
a need of a sharper kind than teaching:
solitary and private, although its fulfillment

depends on the other players who play with her—
all immersed in music instead of words.
But nobody's home tonight. They're probably
all at a concert or recital, some benign event,
probably nothing terrible happened today
to any of them or to the children,
no crippling accident, no hopeless diagnosis,
but the house is so closed and silent it seems dead.

THE USE OF POETRY

On the day a fourteen-year-old disappeared in Ojai, California,
having left a Christmas Eve slumber party barefoot
to "go with a guy" in a green truck,
and all Christmas Day volunteers searched for her body within a fifteen-
     mile radius,
and her father and grandfather searched
and spoke to reporters because TV coverage
might help them find her if she were still alive,
and her mother stayed home with the telephone,
not appearing in public, and I could imagine
this family deciding together this division of labor
and what little else they could do to *do something,*
and the kitchen they sat in, the tones they spoke in,
who cried and who didn't, and how they comforted one another
with words of hope and strokings of backs and necks,
but I couldn't imagine their fear that their daughter
had been murdered in the woods, raped no doubt,
tied up, chopped up, God knows what else,
or them picturing her terror as it was happening to her
or their own terror of her absence ever after,
cut off from them before she had a chance to grow through adolescence,
her room ever the same with its stupid posters of rock stars
until they can bear to take them down
because they can't bear to leave them up anymore—
on this day, which happened to be Christmas,
at the kind of holiday gathering with a whole turkey and spiral-cut ham
and beautiful dishes our hosts spent their money and time making
to cheer their friends and enjoy the pleasure of giving,
in a living room sparkling with scented candles and bunting
and a ten-foot tree adorned with antique ornaments,
the girl's disappearance kept surfacing in conversations across the room
while I was being cornered by a man who said his wife was leaving him
after twenty-one years of marriage, then recited his resumé

as if this couldn't happen to someone with his business acumen;
and it did again after I excused myself to refill my punch glass
when someone at the punch bowl said what she had heard about it from
    someone else
who had played tennis that morning with the girl's mother's doubles
    partner,
while I filled a punch glass for somebody's dad
brought along so he wouldn't be alone on Christmas,
a man in his eighties with a face like a raven's,
his body stooped, ravaged by age and diseases,
who told me he was amazed to still be alive himself
after a year in which he had lost both *his* wife and son,
then, to my amazement, began telling me how important
he is in his business world
just like the man I had just gotten away from,
that he's still a player in international steel
involved in top-drawer projects for the navy,
and I was selfish enough to be selfless enough
to draw him out a little, and the younger man, too
(who appeared at my elbow again and started talking again),
but not selfless enough to feel what they each were going through
because my own fear and hunger
cloud how I imagine everyone,
including the bereaved family of the missing girl,
and the girl herself, and certainly her murderer,
although I know what it is to hate yourself completely
and believe all human community is lies and bullshit
and what happens to other people doesn't matter.

MY OTHER SELF

for Greg and Trish Orr

He could have smacked you
for running out of gas, at midnight,
in December, in a middle-of-nowhere place,
coasting a few sorry yards toward home on the shoulder
as a passing eighteen-wheeler's Hawaiian-sized wave of air
whomped the side of the car like a two-story pillow.
As we sat there immobile—the four of us (including him),
as if waiting for the show to start at a surreal drive-in—
he wanted to reach into the front seat
and bonk your heads together
the way the leader of the Three Stooges did
when the other two did something stupid.
What had been *road* was now a cold place
without a house light in sight in the rural South.
What had been a passionate highway talk
about the culture's indifference to the artist's work
would have been silence except for him
giggling at us, at how danger dissolves discontent
and flashes before us a life lost to pettiness,
which we soon start to lose again.
"What's that adage about wartime curing neurotics?"
he planned to mock us with my voice, but when I got out
to see where we were, he didn't. He brooded in the car.
He didn't feel the pleasure of a skyful of stars
so cold and clear when you look up
its light illuminates your breath.
Nor was he worried about anyone but himself,
being the only one with nothing to worry about,
not made of flesh. He was crying
I wanna go home inside the car
like a child trapped in a junked refrigerator.

This was one time I felt exactly like him,
as we three stood pondering our dilemma calmly, maturely.
And I did again when he yelled *I'm scared*
as the clunker with wide headlights and bad muffler
glided like a crocodile toward our throbbing imported taillights
and idled there. Because I approached the clunker
alone (my other self was having none of this action),
what I found when the window inched down
was reality: a couple with a baby
asleep between them: country people
who still stop for anyone in trouble,
though they were wary. So was I,
squinting into the warm darkness inside their car
as if what might surface was a gun to my face.
They left and came back with a can of gas so fast
their kindness made our entire lives
seem blessed. How lucky we are,
we said on the smooth way home again,
trying to etch it into our brains.
And he would have chimed in
with an impressive disquisition on fortune
if we hadn't ditched him back there
where he still is, thumb out and grinning
into the high beams of every approaching car
since the next one's got to be the starlet in the Jaguar
wrapped in a mink with nothing underneath.

BUNNY

In the scarred desk behind me
in history class,
she lulled her nyloned knee
against my ass,

its message pressing home
as dully we went
from the interminable Fall of Rome
to the Council of Trent

and through the even duller
steel town afternoons,
locked in a collar
of dim green rooms,

old nuns, and ever new
bewilderment.
1962.
Like the hood ornament

on some chopped down hot rod
of the apocalypse,
above the blackboard stood
the crucifix

flanked on either slope
of its tiny Calvary
by color headshots of the Pope
and John F. Kennedy—

an arrangement meant to convey
not thievery being done
but God's work every day
by The Two Johns

drawing us like dynamos
through them to heaven
while we shook in our rows
as if on toboggans.

So what if we had known
what JFK was doing
in Laos and Vietnam,
and who he was screwing

(including the teenage mistress
of the head of the Mafia,
delivered to the White House
like a midnight pizza)?

The greater world to me,
present and past,
was the space between Bunny's knee
and my ass,

and I needed it collapsed
as soon as class began.
So what that I thought she had
the brains of a pecan,

mascara so black and thick
she must have smeared it on
with a popsicle stick,
and a nickname incredibly dumb?

Each day when she had helped me
annihilate an hour,
and we were going away,
I'd stare at her,

and she'd stare back and wink
I know you live off it:
one flashlight blink
at the bottom of a pit.

BIRTHDAY

The years I've lost to selfishness
bivouacked at midnight on my lawn,
aimed an arsenal at the house,
trucked in their dates, and partied til dawn.

They all got plenty drunk enough
to blow the neighborhood to smoke,
but not one touched the lethal guns,
which apparently is the joke

they think they think of when they convene
at the local Motel 6,
where they commandeer the ice machine
and gorge on Cheddar Stix

before the Annual Benefit Brawl
to celebrate the teeth
with which they rip their faces off
and my face underneath.

ASH PIT

St. Louis, 1951

It thumped your sister's skull—
this concrete backyard ash pit—
and changed her face into a flag
of red, branching rivulets

that stopped your game of tag
and her screeches of delight
because she hadn't been It
and she hadn't been caught.

What thrill would she have felt,
this bashful girl of ten,
if her big brother had lunged
and missed her again?

But this time you did not.
The coal in the basement bin
invited you to sit
and think what you had done.

TUTELARY

What a fuckup you are.
What dumbshit you do.
Your father's voice
still whispers in you,

despite the joys
that sweeten each day.
Your Genius it isn't
until, dying away,

it worms back through
the sparkling dream
where you drown him
in an inch-deep stream:

your knee in his back,
your strength on his skull,
it begins singing
praise for your skill.

In the Sink

(Paul H. Ryan, 1909–1964)

Tiny red spider, in your weird world
of instructive vibrations and spikes of heat,
you're spread like a nerve-end naively unfurled
as if my touch would be a treat.

You're safe for now, at least from me—
although your utter otherness
mocks my being who I don't want to be,
because it's only obvious

you're the one stuck in a porcelain bowl
where any drunk who wants a drink
could send you swirling down a hole
and never see you in the sink.

Influence is too pale a word
for how a father lives in his son.
Rejoice you're not his drop of blood.
I'd flick this faucet and be Gone.

BALLAD OF THE FOUR LAST THINGS

Death, Judgement, Heaven, Hell

I flew from dorm to dorm to dorm
looking for a bed.
I mean *flew,* through walls and doors,
as if already dead.

I said flew through walls and doors
but no door was locked to me.
The rooms were square and dark and spare,
furnished monastically.

I don't know where the students were.
I saw no one until
having searched a hundred rooms
she was lying still

as judgement, in an upper bunk,
hoping I wouldn't see.
But upright we were face to face
and hers showed pity of me.

I apologized for bringing her
my terror and my dread.
I said I'm so tired, I need to sleep.
"It's all right," she said.

Then I *was* sleeping in a room alone
a big man broke into
and woke me as I had awakened her.
What was he going to do?

CHRONIC SEVERE INCURABLE

There's nothing more you can learn from pain,
but here it comes again—with its monotone,
its idiot drone, like a brick wall against which
thinking smacks its big skull until it's juiceless
fruit the devil reams clean with red teeth
and razor-blade tongue. Pain:
payment, penalty, punish, revenge—
all these miseries inhering in the word:
you must think no word for what you feel.
The being pain is being is you.

Mr. Pain Speaks for Himself

That I love you you can't
deny because you think
you don't love me. Each day
I drive you to the brink

as faithfully as mom
her precious little one
to soccer, dance, and violin.
Don't you get it, hon?

I'm not going anywhere,
but you are. So when
you feel me rolling in
like a fleet of Peterbilts,

don't try to run away again
like a watermelon on stilts,
but love me and be changed
to what you can't imagine.

GOD

Maybe you're a verb, or some
lost part of speech
that would let us talk sense
instead of monkey-screech

when we try to explain you
to our loved ones and ourselves
when we most need to.
Who knows why someone dies

in the thick of happiness,
his true love finally found,
the world showering success
as if the world were only a cloud

that floated in a dream
above a perfect day?
Are you also dreaming our words?
Give us something to say.

for D. B.

WINGS OF THE MORNING

She says her heart is ripped
because of him, and he
might reply he tried to help her see
before their life together stopped

and he gave up: Just look
at all these *things* you bought!
he was about to shout,
as if the deep-glazed vase she took

time and attention to find
and place here to show
dawn light through their window
could seem to shine for him

had been responsible for what
his life is not — like these filmy
curtains that constantly beautifully
shape the breeze they caught.

TRIBUTE

I can't give the king
nothing but eggs, I thought
waking up. Deeply you slept
beneath the predawn light,

barely a half-lumen
all sponged up around you
by the white, white bed.
Your hair, I swear, is golden

and your face bones so fine,
but you were the grave mound
into which I could never weep enough
just then.

Why here why now why us
granted this fragile happiness?
I swore I'd use it scrupulously,
if only he'd spare your life.

FLIMSY

Last night I got shot in the head
as I often do: this one
point blank temple soft spot
from the handgun of a man

who broke into my motel
because the flimsy door lock
would not lock. Oh well,
whatever heart-bursting terror

I'm supposed to learn in dreams
could be useful someday
when a beloved voice screams
and life changes utterly.

No one's immune.
It's happening to someone now.
The police, the ambulance,
these strangers in the house.

THE OTHERS

They slept and ate like us.
Feral they were not.
The intricacy of their handiwork
bespoke a fineness we'd be taught.

Yet we wiped them out.
It was eerily easy to do,
although they knew we were coming
and knew we knew they knew.

Not only did they not resist
our guns like bloody hacking coughs
in their libraries and hospitals,
their bedrooms and their schools—

they would not acknowledge us.
We felt like fools. There was no keening.
Even the children did not cry.
It was as if meaning

inhered so deeply in their daily
lives we could not touch it;
nor would they quit living to be
slaughtered, it was so inviolate.

A GOOD FATHER

The cancer's eaten half his liver.
The bile's going to the brain.
With one night more at most to live,
he's acting insane.

The food his family brings is poison.
Not one of them has ever cared.
What a life he would have lived without them,
if only he'd dared.

Conversations while he's sleeping—
in the hallway, on the phone—
link his dear ones in forgiveness
while he alone

joins the torments of resentment
swelling to its highest power
that will take him like a whirlwind
across the river of fire.

EVERY SUNDAY

Psychotic homeless boy
blocking our exit from the church—
straggle-haired, bloated,
eyes shining like ice—

doing his rooster-pecking thing
with his hand made the beak
into each of our faces
as we file out—

or is it snake-striking
or airhole-punching
or just compulsive counting us
one and one and one?

He will not live long.
He will allow the pastor
to wrap an arm around his shoulder,
and lead him to coffee and crullers.

But to *be* him

A Dead Girl

Where were joy and grace
when your dad would shout,
"What are you—stupid?"
and slap you on the mouth

for the steak you overcooked
or the egg you underfried?
They were not in that house
nor anyone inside

but seemed to live downtown
with the funny guy you liked
who liked the way you looked
in dog collars and spikes

before he took you under the pier
to meet some men he knew
and you went as in a dream
to see what had been waiting for you.

DISTANT FRIEND

To have a friendship with a guy
you could blow enthusiastically
once a week seems to you
the height of intimacy

to which you may legitimately
aspire, as if by aiming low
you'll hit upon someone to love.
I don't think so,

and, when I say, "It doesn't work that way,"
a glaring like the sun
issues from your eyes. But you reply,
"Oh well, at least it'd be fun,"

meaning (politely) End Of Discussion.
You're right: I was presumptuous
to speak as if I know the possibilities
for happiness, much less

for someone who has always known
he will always be alone.

DICKHEAD

A man who's trying to be a good man
but isn't, because he can't not take
whatever's said to him as judgement.
It causes him, as he puts it, to *react*.
His face and neck redden and bloat,
a thick blue vein bulges up his forehead
and bisects his bald pate, scaring his children
but provoking hilarity at work
where one guy likes to get his goat
by pasting pro-choice bumper stickers
on his computer screen while he's in the john,
then gathers a group into the next cubicle
to watch when he comes back.
He has talked to his minister and to his wife
about learning how not to *react,*
to make a joke, and he has tried to make jokes,
but his voice gets tense, they come out flat,
so even his joke becomes a joke at his expense,
another thing to laugh at him about.
He has thought to turn to them and ask,
Why don't you like me? What have I done to you?
But he has been told already all his life:
self-righteous goody two-shoes, a stick up your ass.
They are right. He has never never never gotten along.
He says nothing this time, just peels off the bumper sticker,
crumples it gently, places it gently
by his mousepad to dispose of later properly,
comparing his suffering to Christ's in Gethsemane
spat upon and mocked (his minister's advice),
and tries a smile that twists into a grimace,
which starts the hot blood rising into his face.
This is what they came for, to see Dickhead,
the bulging vein, the skull stoplight-red,

and indeed it is remarkable how gorged it gets
as if his torso had become a helium pump,
so, except for him whose eyes are shut tight,
they burst into laughter together exactly at the moment
cruelty turns into astonishment.

COMPLETE SEMEN STUDY

morphology: "pinheads": 2 percent

Laborious, stumpy, droopy, askew,
blundering into one another
while the healthy sperm zips by like the varsity water polo team
on their way to a party with the best-looking cheerleaders—
unbeautiful losers, unfittest and unmourned,
o my five-hundred-thousand-or-so pinheads
floundering in this plastic cup's murky bottom,
what would *you* do to be half of someone?
Wank it sitting on the toilet in a fluorescent
pea-green hospital bathroom while learning to juggle one-handed
one cup and three brown-bagged *Penthouses*
offered by the deadpan female lab attendant?
You'd wank it anyplace, I think.
They'd tie your wrists if you had wrists
to stop your rubbing off on fireplugs and brick buildings,
much less on a hand's elastic flesh
you're too dim to recognize is your own.
You're the ones who can't be taken to church
because you hump the pew cushions
while the rest of us are praying,
and try to straddle the priest's leg like a puppy
while he exchanges an inspirational word or two
with each of his congregation as they file from the service.
I, on the other hand, am too mature for this.
The Pet-of-the-Month could almost be my granddaughter.
My metabolism has decelerated
to that of an elderly Galápagos Tortoise.
I could do very well all day sunning myself
under a thick, warm shell, and could easily take the next century
to burn the calories in a slice of pizza.
In the world for which my body was designed
I would have checked out long ago,

immolated at the ritual bonfire by my two hundred great-grandchildren
roasting a mammoth in my honor,
dancing for days stoned on sacred leaf juice,
and intermarrying like howler monkeys in the bushes.
It's no doubt due to nights like this
that you weakened and malformed
and chase your own watery tails until you decompose
into what the complete semen study classifies as "debris."
The doctors say it's age or car exhaust or groundwater toxins
or they-don't-know-what, but eons ago there must have been a boy
waiting for the dopey old patriarch to die
so he could do his sister sweaty and writhing in the firelight.
If their child, slow-witted and guileless,
showed the endearing but useless gift
to greet everyone's spirit no matter their status,
they might have thrown him the bones the dogs had finished with,
which is how they fed the shunned and the shamed,
unbeautiful losers, unfittest and unmourned,
o my five-hundred-thousand-or-so pinheads
floundering in this plastic cup's murky bottom
I hereby hand over for removal and disposal
to the now surgically gloved
deadpan female lab attendant.

ESCHATOLOGY

The dead are too quick for us.
That look of distance on their faces
the instant after the last breath—
it's because they have already traveled light-years away.
It doesn't matter how they die
or who they were while alive:
they've earned the Presidential Suite
in the Five-Star Resort at the edge of the expanding universe.
They are, in fact, the reason the universe expands,
because there are always more of them,
which keeps the developers busy,
which keeps employment up, inflation down, and investment growing,
so the economy keeps expanding, too.
What's good for the dead is good for the country.
Check out the serial killer who died by lethal injection.
No, the one with water wings
about to splash Joseph Goebbels off his float.
He couldn't get over being sodomized with a beer bottle
and the canned dog food they made him eat afterward, but look at him now:
a fun person, well adjusted, a useful citizen.
He doesn't get mad about anything anymore, much less homicidal.
That's his parents, waving from the thatch-roofed bar by the pool,
enjoying a mai-tai, which they can now take or leave.
All the dead are like this: serene.
God is merciful. He knows being human was hellish enough,
chased by the Thousand Fears down all those blind alleys
the Buddhists teach are nothing but attachment
to hunger, sex, the need to be touched—
rampant appetites repeatedly frustrated and our physical perception
so sluggish we can't see the dead are exactly like us
except they want nothing but what they are given,
love one another unselfishly, and are
always laughing uproariously, having a great time.

Extended Care

I'm not ready to write my last poems—
paeans to the glory of sun porch and duck pond
and inner peace that comes to me at last
when, out of terror, I begin to pray incessantly
and love all my neighbors as I love myself,
including the unknown one who steals my crackers
and the former state senator who sings
"God Bless America" for every meal and snack time.
I'll have to be ninety plus, maybe over a hundred,
nine-tenths blind and needing a fresh diaper,
before my blinding fear of losing and not-getting
lifts like the huge purple curtain at the Metropolitan Opera
to reveal the extraordinary blessings of an ordinary day.
Maybe my hearing will also be so far gone
that I finally understand the voices in my head
debating whether or not I deserve to live,
when in fact—I'll realize—I'm living okay right now,
although I may still believe life could be better
if someone installed a lock on my snack box
and gave that state senator a laryngectomy.
How lovely (I'll think) every person I've known.
Even the egocentric shitheels had a kind of charm,
and the ones who lied purposely to cause me damage—
maybe they had kids they loved or parents they took care of.
They surely did nothing worse than the worst things I did.
Everyone will appear to me as a scarred soul
struggling with the same sort of torments and disappointments,
as death rises like a dinosaur out of the duck pond
and lumbers dripping toward me on the sun porch
where I glow with the modest good I did with my life,
grateful this gorgeous world will be here for others when I am gone.

Dream Pun on "Single Man"
Before Marrying Again

I don't know how I knew
the signalman was the signalman.
His fuzzy red-brown hair
the color of blood? I knew
he wasn't just a waiter carrying a tray
when he pushed through the rathskeller
doing the Hitler salute—not straight up
Sieg Heil but the lateral one,
elbow-fulcrum on his shoulder's plane,
hand (made into blade) starting at his heart
sweeping the quadrant in front of him
as if only to clear a path
through the jolly, blocked aisle.

You weren't the woman I was eating with
at the tall table
where we watch the sky change
at sunset and talk about our day
(characters from each other's lives
flickering ghostlike through that intimate air)—
nor could I hear what she said anymore
when he pushed through doing the Hitler salute
that meant run right then to save myself.
There wasn't time for a word to her.
The bomb exploded as I got out the door.

You know what it was like in there.
You've listened to me so many hours
depicting aftermaths of my blunt shame.
The place had been jammed, everyone drunk,
the cellar had kept the explosion in—
pillowed, muffled, a brief hot thud

within thick earth-sunk concrete walls.
But oh my God what it had done.
I crawled back into the rubble
searching for her, until I saw
the work I had to do now.
What I had done was done,
I'd never know how. I had to help with
the wounded and haul out the dead.

An Old Book in Florence

Ancient Art and Ritual by Jane Ellen Harrison, London, 1913

It smells like water from a rusty pump
I drank as a child on my grandmother's farm
in Bellflower, Missouri—this old book
from a British subscription library in Italy.
The water it absorbed from basement air
minute by minute, year after year,
browned the edges of the pages
and fades toward their centers to a faint rust color;
specks of darker rust blot words and letters;
and, on the insides of both covers,
squiggles the shade of dried blood
have made a kind of topographical map
that shows only rivers.
A modern scanning x-ray machine
might have seen a splinter of flame
like a votive candle in the underground stacks,
and the book salvaged with sponges
and tweezers and chemicals.
But no technology can save it now:
the touch of its paper is the skin of hands
dried out by work and crosshatched with veins.

The life it had was in people's hands.
Someone's earnest marginalia
by someone almost erased—
fragments of a dead man's opinion
in a book that's almost dust—
but they must have been alive in him
when he returned the book
to the British Institute and stepped
out onto a gray stone street in Florence
bordered by a wall where you can rest your elbows

and watch the river change with the light
like heavy shot silk. Here's
one passage in the book he marked:
"It's what the tribe feels that is sacred.
One may make by himself excited movements,
he may leap for joy, for fear;
but unless these movements are made by the tribe
together, they will not become rhythmical;
they will probably lack intensity
and certainly permanence."
To this he shouted "No!" in the margin,
addressing the author, Jane Ellen Harrison:
"Madame, you are an islander as I am."

In our family, my grandmother was famed
for gentle toughness that yielded to no one.
In 1913, a teenage bride on an Ozark dirt farm—
did her life already somehow contain
the deaths of her husband and son,
my father, who had just been born?
I had heard the phrase "gentle toughness" spoken
by grownups when she left the table after holiday meals,
and spoken by my parents in the dashboard-lit
front seat during the long car rides back to St. Louis,
and I understood what *they* meant by it,
but to me "gentle toughness" was the way her hands felt
when she passed me the dented tin cup
to hold under the spout while she pumped,
saying "Look for bugs before you drink!"
before she'd rough my cheek and tell me
I was her special one. Often as not,
there would be a fat red beetle
floating in the cup, which she'd pinch out

and hold right up to my nose—
its six tiny thorny legs still trying to swim in air—
and say, "That's never going to hurt you"
and flick it away like a speck of lint.
Then she'd tell me I could drink, and that's when
I'd tip the cup and smell the water
and see the silver bottom battered into craters
and drinking was being face to face with the moon.

A VERSION OF HAPPINESS

for Ellen Bryant Voigt

Tonight the band's Nigerian—
Afro-Cuban, last week; next week, Cajun:
the summer multicultural concert series
in the San Juan Capistrano library courtyard;
two hundred of us, all ages, in the audience;
Edenic evening air and stars: tickets six bucks.
You'd love this music, this place:
the musicians are like poets (they have day jobs)
and they're *good:* they play this music
because they love it, love making it,
love being able to make it—together
(unlike poets?). The sound
each is part of and takes part in
feeds through their collective body
into the next chord and phrase—
into fingers, lips, lungs, even elbows
in the case of the maniac-god on the congas
when guitars and horns cease
and lead singers politely step aside
so that we may witness his five-minute solo
and feel, as they do, the triumph of prowess
over human clumsiness, and notice
who's drumming us into this happy trance.
Now they give us this chance: to notice.
They eye us like parents watching children
unwrap gifts. He sweats not only for us
but also for what against all reason he can do
with whapping palms and shuttling elbows
that engender exponentially beyond his allotted
two of each, because how can one man do this?
Ancient our amazement and this power
that has caused sane men to run point-blank into fusillades

or shuttle themselves, their wives, and their postmarital
extra twenty pounds behind a column of the courtyard portico
to dance beside an eleven-year-old and her mom.
All evening these two have been a joy to notice:
the girl goofing with her dancing, freckled, gangly,
her mom I imagine still her best friend
before the teenage hormonal tsunami sweeps her away
like a beach shack. Mom's late-thirtyish,
bespectacled, frumpy, doing dorky disco moves (like me)
she probably learned riding *her* tsunami
in front of a mirror to Bee Gees songs
with an inconsolable crush on John Travolta
and no clue that happiness might come
someday from a parental talent for pleasure
in what a child can do. I know
your father thought your playing piano for the choir
in Baptist churches in rural Virginia
the pinnacle of achievement.
He loved music but couldn't play it,
so he wanted you to, and you did.
How extreme a child's love is. I guess
we'll do anything to make our parents love us
even if they can't. The ones who can,
though . . .—ludicrous of me
to try to put in words what it does to be loved
like that, but it's still visible
in you, my dear friend. This frumpy mom
shows it, too, as does her girl
despite trials, heartbreaks, and disasters
she may have already and certainly will suffer.
Nobody gets out alive, except in spirit
(the lucky ones), which as you know
can grow through music that couldn't be more
bodily, but translates beautifully.

A French Café in Orange County

on our Tenth Anniversary

If I could track the converging forces
that put me here, they'd culminate
with you who go for milky coffee in bowls
and croissants big as couch pillows, but where
would they begin? I mean before
something congealing in the Ur–bacteria soup
began to yearn for some other congealing thing.
Yearning to please the beloved
compounds that first felt urge, I think—
even if God didn't plan it that way for Himself
when He yearned for the world
and it instantly emerged from nothingness
as a difficult Beauty to deal with.
Despite what we've been through since,
there are still such moments of grace
when we see each other in the old light
when it was all just chemistry and promise—
the promise, we found out, to each be changed
by how we each had to change to stay together,
as love made us the persistent
mysteries to each other we became.

REMINDER

Torment by appetite
is itself an appetite
dulled by inarticulate,
dogged, daily

loving-others-to-death—
as Chekhov put it, "compassion
down to your fingertips"—
looking on them as into the sun

not in the least for their sake
but slowly for your own
because it causes
the blinded soul to bloom

like deliciousness in dirt,
like beauty from hurt,
their light—*their* light—
pulls so surely. Let it.